Group Motion
in Practice

Group Motion in Practice

Collective Creation Through Dance Movement Improvisation

BRIGITTA HERRMANN *and*
MANFRED FISCHBECK
with ELIA A. SINAIKO *and* ANNA BERESIN

McFarland & Company, Inc., Publishers
Jefferson, North Carolina

ISBN (print) 978-1-4766-7278-6
ISBN (ebook) 978-1-4766-3209-4

LIBRARY OF CONGRESS CATALOGUING DATA ARE AVAILABLE

BRITISH LIBRARY CATALOGUING DATA ARE AVAILABLE

© 2018 Brigitta Herrmann and Manfred Fischbeck. All rights reserved

No part of this book may be reproduced or transmitted in any form or by any means, electronic or mechanical, including photocopying or recording, or by any information storage and retrieval system, without permission in writing from the publisher.

Front cover image of Group Activation Dance, Group Motion Retreat at Crestone Mountain Zen Center, CO (photograph Colin Harvey); *background* © 2018 scibak/iStock

Printed in the United States of America

McFarland & Company, Inc., Publishers
Box 611, Jefferson, North Carolina 28640
www.mcfarlandpub.com

To our daughters Laina and Aura
and to the future of dance on this planet.
—Brigitta Herrmann and Manfred Fischbeck

Table of Contents

Acknowledgments   ix
Preface   1
Introduction   3
   The Origins of Group Motion   3
   Group Motion in Practice   6
   Dance Is My Life: Brigitta's Story   8
   Running into Dance: Manfred's Story   20
   Group Motion Performance Stories   30

Part I. Group Motion Game Structures   33

Solo/Duet   34
Active-Passive   34
Activation   38
Mirror   40
Closing Your Eyes   42
Self Portrait Dance   42
Solo Dance/Writing   43
Dialogue   45
Connected to Strings   46
Self-Activation   47
Breathing Movement   49
*Final Reflections on Solo/
   Duet Forms*   50

Circle   55
Impulse   55
Name Game   57
Adding   58
*Final Reflections on Circle
   Forms*   61

Space   64
Areas   64
Crystallization   65
The Grid   67
Shadow Dance   69
Exchange Game   72
Moving or Being Still   73
Triangle/Diamond Dance   74
*Group Dialogue/Trialogue
   Dance*   77
*Final Reflections on Space
   Forms*   78

Sound   82
Time Dance   82
Message Dance   84
Receiving Sound Energy   85
Conducting Sound Energy   87
*Sound Activation/
   Soundscapes*   89

Words into Sounds 90
Final Reflections on Sound Forms 91

WORD 94
Traveling Landscapes 94
Say What You Do 97
Word/Movement Mirror 98
Chat Room 99
Writing Process and Activation 100
Textography 102
Storytelling Dance 104
Alter Ego Monologue 105
Alter Ego Dialogue 105
Final Reflections on Word Forms 107

RITUAL 111
House or Village Square Dance 111
Object Dance 113
Group Activations 116
Tableaux Stills 116
Group Tableaux Travel 117
Evolution Cycle 118
Past Lives Circle 119
Doing Nothing: The Dance of Stillness 120
Game Sequences 121
Introduction to the Friday Night Workshop 122
Model of Group Motion on a Friday Night 123
The Significance of Ritual Dances 131

Part II. Group Motion Practices   141
Eight Therapeutic Principles of Group Motion 142
The Partnership of Dance and Music 148
A Process of Collective Creation 151
Community Performance Project 155
Monday Night Improv Lab 157
Moving Beyond the Games 158
Reflection on the Practice of Free Improvisation 161
Practice of Interaction with Technology 164

Part III. Closing Conversations and Meditations   167
Cooperation: The Universal Creative Principle 168
Dance as a Vehicle for Understanding Human Nature 168
The Awakening of the Body in the Technological Age 169
The Art of Dance and Transformation 174
The Art of Free Improvisation 174
From Then to Now and There to Here 175
Dance as an Art Form 177
Dance Is a Way of Life 178

Appendix I: Dance Chronology: Brigitta Herrmann   181
Appendix II: Theater and Dance Chronology: Manfred Fischbeck   185
Bibliography   189
Index   191

Acknowledgments

The Group Motion dance is like a tree with many branches, leaves and flowers that for over 50 years of growing has withstood the elements of weather—thriving, wilting, blooming, drooping, flourishing, waning, prospering and multiplying—on an ongoing odyssey of love and perseverance. And the roots, a fractal mirror image of the outer branches and leaves, reemerge throughout the pages of this book.

Our thanks to you, the Dancing Tribe on Friday Nights, which has spread in all the dancing places around the world, and to all the dancers, movers, music makers and artists from near and far away, too many to name, in the thousands. We love you all!

Additional thanks to all who lent assistance to this book by writing, reviewing, encouraging, contributing, and believing in seeing it done:

Jim Punkre for reviewing, contributing, encouraging the book in progress,

Nina Sherak for clarifying, editing assistance and encouragement in the process,

Djuna Wojton for years of support and the first video production of Group Motion workshop,

Andrea Clearfield for promoting, supporting and initiating Group Motion workshops and retreats,

Alden and Dolores Josey for creating and offering the Port Clyde Conference Center as a retreat for Group Motion workshops,

Laura and Micah Bertin who believed and nourished it, for holding the space for the Group Motion Workshop on the Main Line,

Past and present members of our "dancing board," Carol Hinzman, Harold Katz, Megan Murphy King, Patty Redenbaugh, Peter Sody, Stacey Meadows and Miriam Giguere,

Long-time Group Motion community members, supporters and contributors to the book Gary Gray, Doris Ferleger, Diane Hetrick, Kristin Narcowich,

Musicians Ron Kravitz, David Ford, Robert Rudnitsky, Loyd Bashkin, Mostafa Mouhib, and Tim Motzer for their ongoing passionate and committed musical support of the Friday Night Workshop,

and Bill Hebert, Colin Harvey and Richard Marcus, Harold Jacobs, Matthew Sharp, and Margie Politzer for the generous provision of photos and videos.

We thank our daughters, Laina and Aura, for their powerful, spirited vision and generous display of dance, and for the dynamic spreading of the Group Motion Workshop both nationally and internationally. We thank them for their devotion to Group Motion, for their enduring love, and for giving and empowering dance through performing, choreographing, and teaching.

We would also like to thank these organizations for supporting us and Group Motion with awards and grants over the years: The National Endowment for the Arts, the Pennsylvania Council on the Arts, the Philadelphia Culture Fund, The Pew Center for Arts and Heritage, the William Penn Foundation, Dance Advance, WHYY, the Philadelphia Dance Collection, the Independence Foundation, the Samuel S. Fels Fund, the First Person Arts, the Mid Atlantic Arts Foundation, and the US/Japan Friendship Commission. Thanks also to: Arcosanti, Arizona; the Crestone Mountain Zen Center, Colorado; and the Community Education Center, Philadelphia for providing homes for the Group Motion Workshop for many years.

Finally, we thank the University of the Arts for providing funding towards the completion of this book.

Preface

Group Motion is both a performance company and a movement improvisation practice with the same name, based on the company's philosophy, developed in workshops of choreographic experimentation, and now outlined in this historical guidebook. This volume reflects 50 years of co-creation between dancers, choreographers, teachers Brigitta Herrmann and Manfred Fischbeck, along with the participation of thousands of dancers, musicians, videographers and ordinary, extraordinary people who have danced, played, and performed with them around the world.

Part memoir, part guidebook, part philosophy of art treatise, the book in your hand can be read for its stories, for its games, for inspiration. It does not offer a general history of improvisation in dance; instead, it presents a personal and original history of the evolution and elevation of dance improv through Group Motion. It does not place Group Motion's history within a formal history of dance performance, although you will find many performances described here. The book offers insight into the study of professional dance, but more importantly it encourages practicing movement as a means to living an expressive and gratifying life.

Rooted in Mary Wigman's German expressionist dance, and informed by other contemporary dance and theater traditions, Group Motion evolved and now represents a particular form of improvisational performance practice, one not merely emphasizing the singular creative potential of the individual, but the creative interchange within a group. Here you will find step-by-step guidance for dozens of improvisational structures presented as games, useful for enhancing group dynamics and creating instant choreographies. Group Motion's vision has brought improv performance not only onto stages, but into prisons, airports, and public parks. From the importance of individual expression to group consciousness and creativity, from an ancient sense of ritual dance to the incorporation of technology in post-modern performance, Group Motion embodies what anthropologist Victor Turner called "the human seriousness of play," and the primacy of movement as an expressive language.

Brigitta Herrmann and Manfred Fischbeck met the writer Elia Sinaiko while Group Motion was in residency at Antioch College. Elia recognized the healing potential of their practices, which he felt could be adapted for use. It was his idea to begin the process of writing a guidebook to the game structures. He recalls,

> It is hard to say who of us was most naive: I by asking them to accept a stranger for such an intimate purpose, or they for accepting one. But through our immediate trust, this book was begun.
>
> I was soon to find out that to Manfred and Brigitta, Group Motion was above all, an art form, part of a revolution in art in which the person is the form. I came to realize that in the broadest sense of art and therapy, the two overlap, and in Group Motion, they can, and often do, become one. It is exactly because each person can so intimately become the art that he is creating, that he can express from within himself something especially beautiful.

In Group Motion, dance "form" refers to shape and format: solo, duet, circle, triangle, crystal. It can also refer to sounds and words, and even ritual. These are choreographic terms. Smaller form categories include things like following and leading, giving and receiving. Structures and games are built within and around forms. Whether something is a structure or game depends on the way it functions, socially and choreographically. Structures and games are experiences and depend on contexts. Soccer is a structure with rules, but it is played as a game. Dance has form, structure, and typically with Group Motion, game.

Play scholar Anna Beresin came onboard in 2014, after working with Manfred as a faculty member at The University of the Arts in Philadelphia. Having just written a book called *The Art of Play,* she served as editor for this project, meeting often with Brigitta and Manfred to collaborate. Anna had used their game structures in her work with children and recognized the need for a Group Motion guidebook to improvisation. The book took shape as it became clear that the Group Motion method was rooted in the collective creation of its participants, and the unique circumstances of Manfred and Brigitta's lives, presented here as a fusion of practice and biography.

Introduction

The Origins of Group Motion

Founded in 1962 by Brigitta Herrmann, Hellmut Gottschild, and Katharina Sehnert, Motion Berlin was a chamber dance company evolving from the Mary Wigman School of Dance. One of the few independent modern dance companies in Germany at the time, the company performed throughout the country and in Europe. In 1967, Manfred Fischbeck, co-director of an independent Berliner theater group, "Provisorisches Theater," or Temporary Theater, joined the company for the creation of *Countdown for Orpheus*, their first multimedia production, combining text, film, set, live music, and improvisation in performance. In 1968, Brigitta Herrmann, Hellmut Gottschild, and Manfred Fischbeck moved to the United States and re-formed in Philadelphia as the contemporary modern dance company Group Motion, a pioneer in the development of multimedia dance theater.

A New York debut brought instant acknowledgment and critical acclaim.

> The form of the dancers is open, cool, jagged, but their dancing is so full-blooded that, watching them, you are often on the edge of your seat with a kind of sympathetic, kinetic tension.... Group Motion in effect puts hot movement into cool contexts.—*Village Voice*

> The company has hold of an exceptionally interesting idea ... that of organic group movement.—*New York Times*

Group Motion quickly received critical recognition, performing at Judson Church in New York and at Jacob's Pillow Dance Festival in 1969, as well as joining the National Endowment for the Arts touring program. Gottschild left the company in 1971 to found Zero Moving Company, while Fischbeck and Herrmann continued as co-directors. In 1971, Herrmann and Fischbeck created the Group Motion Workshop, an outgrowth of their work with the company. Since then, the company and the workshop have toured nationally and abroad, traveling through Germany, France, Argentina, Barbados, Japan, Taiwan, Poland and Lithuania in addition to performing regularly at their home base in Philadelphia. Each week, Group Motion continues to conduct the acclaimed Friday Night Workshop at the Community Education Center in West Philadelphia.

At the core of Group Motion's work lives the vision of dance as a language of expression and communication accessible to anyone. From that idea, different forms of creative dance movement practices, teaching techniques, and structures of improvisation have evolved over fifty years. The improvisational structures and games described in this book, those created in the context of Group Motion, and those adapted from other sources, provide the essential building blocks of the work.

Within the life of Group Motion, the Friday Night Workshop has been and continues to be at the heart of the creative practice. The format of a guided improvisational dance movement ritual with live music, open to all, was created in the early seventies and has been an ongoing event every Friday night since. As a meeting ground for dancers and non-dancers, musicians, artists, people of all ages and professions and from all walks of life, the Friday Night Workshop has held a ritual space of building community and celebrating dance. Over the years, it has served thousands of people and it continues to thrive and grow as a place for self-expression and play, healing and transformation.

The games served as an essential part of Group Motion's educational offerings: from children's classes and performances to workshops and assembly programs in schools, from master classes in technique and improvisation to curricula in improvisation and composition at colleges and universities. They have been used in psychiatric hospitals, senior centers, youth prisons, and schools for the physically challenged and with children of special needs. The interactive, creative, play inducing and performative community-building nature of the games has proven to be successful in all of these different contexts, for individuals with any level of movement experience.

From the beginning the Group Motion approach to improv has been developed and applied to the company's dance process in variety of ways. The games serve as teaching and learning tools in training practice, as well as tools to experiment with choreography. Frequently the practice is incorporated into performances as structured improvisation or in combination with choreography. On occasion, an invitation to participate in improvisation is extended to the audience at the end of a performance. Some performances are entirely based on improvisation, either with the backbone of a score, or no score at all, but always accompanied by live improvised music in the spirit of collaborative creation.

Initially created as a method to create instant choreographic patterns and images in performance, the exercises turned out to offer much more than that. Their playful, creative, non-competitive nature, proved to be an applicable and productive tool with groups of people, large or small, willing to be guided to play and interact on this basic human level of the language of movement.

This book shares Group Motion structured improvisation in the form of games, along with reflections, conversations, and testimonies of participants and spectators. The personal stories are here to give the reader insights into the emergence of this work, its essential reason to be, and to highlight how the intimate connections between the personal and professional lives of its creators built the base for a process of collective creation.

Cultures and Species, Group Motion Company performance at Arts Bank, Philadelphia, Pennsylvania, 2001. Left to right: David Konyk, Emily Hubler (lying down), Megan Bridge, Kathryn McNamara, Lesya Popil (photograph courtesy Bill Hebert).

Lung-Ta (The Windhorse), Group Motion Company performance at the Painted Bride Art Center, Philadelphia, Pennsylvania, 2008. *Left to right:* Shannon Murphy, Lindsay Browning, Sara Yassky (clasping J. Luna's hand), Hedy Wyland, John Luna and Marie Brown (photograph courtesy Bill Hebert).

Group Motion in Practice

Part I. Group Motion Game Structures

Here the structures are offered in a format of play, with guidance on how to experiment with improv in a variety of games. This technique integrates highly refined approaches to improvisation, incorporating principles of yoga, contact dance, conscious breathing and voice. The games are organized into categories that describe the essence of each structure: Solo/Duet, Circle, Space, Sound, Word, and Ritual.

The games encourage empathy and spontaneous exchange among participants of a group. They also create an opportunity to relate to others in a number of ways, often presenting a choice to be active or passive, to lead or to follow, to give or receive, an experience that is further enriched with the reversal of roles.

The games are not entirely free-form. Elia Sinaiko points out,

> Group Motion calls them games because they are played with rules. However, they differ from common games in one essential way: they are not competitive. Their objective is to communicate, to celebrate, to create or recreate through playing. The rules of the games make possible a creative sharing, providing enough structure and still allowing enough freedom for the dancers to express themselves.

In their simplicity on the one hand, and complexity on the other, these games have been proven to be true and perfect forms, devices to exchange energy, rituals to experience and celebrate the connection between all forms of movement and life. These games can be played on all levels of technical and physical ability, by dancers and "non-dancers" alike. It is not a technique that the games rely on, but rather a truthfulness with oneself and one's own experience.

The Group Motion games were developed through observation and experience of these forms as natural communication, manifested in the movements of the human body. They are based on the basic dynamic of active and passive roles, whether it is leading or following, mirroring, or joining. Most, if not all of these forms are analogous to phenomena of communication in nature. The Triangle Game resembles the flocking of birds, the Impulse Game is based on the principle of chain reaction. Some even make the analogy apparent in their title, like the Mirror or the Crystallization Games.

To speak with our bodies, we have to learn or relearn their languages. All human beings have the same bodily structure, in spite of our distinct individual differences. We are bound to have the same basic movement vocabulary, a common understanding that goes beyond the most basic functions of walking, running, sitting, an inborn knowledge of the signs and signals of the body, and of the inborn principles of communication that are inherent to their systems. It also becomes clear that there is also a commonality with other forms of life, other organizations of energy and matter. All principles of communication seem to be based on one formula—that of giving and receiving, active/passive, output/input, exhale and inhale, expansion and contraction. It is important to allow the dancers to warm up and to become centered before the game improvisations begin. They should take a moment to meditate, to be still, and to empty their minds, to ready themselves for what emerges.

Part II. Group Motion Practices

Group Motion practices aim to provide a visual, auditory, and kinesthetic sharpening of perception in relation to others. Immediate and spontaneous creativity, and especially creativity of the body has a personal value that goes beyond that of dance in performance. By centering ourselves, and learning to recognize our true impulses and the impulses of others, we can gain a greater measure of self and self-expression. Spontaneously, following these real impulses, we feel free. We take away social anxieties and replace them with real communication by learning to speak and live creatively with our bodies. Thus, in a culture that has gradually alienated itself from a healthy approach to touch and physical interaction, a culture rushed in time, Group Motion offers a therapeutic, nurturing, and healing aesthetic experience.

Part III. Closing Conversations and Meditations

The ability to create dialogue through these interactive structures, and to function in small and in large groups—up to two hundred people—goes beyond the common understanding of dance performance. The book concludes with meditations and conversations about dance and improvisation itself, not just for the dance educator, or dancer performer, but for all, as a guide to vibrant living.

Appendices include the performance chronologies of both Brigitta Herrmann and Manfred Fischbeck, and the end of this introduction begins with each of their stories of a living a life defined by dance, to be followed by a brief collection of Group Motion performance stories.

Dance Is My Life: Brigitta's Story

Dance, as I was taught it when I began, meant to put on black tights and leotards, spotless and intact, your hair tightened to your head, and to hold on to the bar, bending and straightening your legs to the point of exhaustion, learning steps, as if you have never been able to walk before, feeling your body as if it were stumbling, tensing to the point of being breathless.

I believe that this is still the way of learning for many who desire to dance today: struggling with one's body, starting to dislike its shape, its imperfections, desiring to have the body fit an image of beauty, comparing oneself with the image in the mirror. Much to the contrary was the teaching of Mary Wigman, who I was graced to study with for six years. In her teaching, she was able to bring alive the impulse of dance in her students. She was able to reach the soul and to free the mind from limiting thoughts. There, I continued learning to dance through experiencing it as a way of speaking, and as a way of spontaneous expression, as a form of communication. It was the learning of dance through improvisation. This way of learning to dance conveyed to me what dance is truly about: dance as language, as a direct possibility to access inner realities spontaneously, as a medium of the moment. The instrument is the human body, with all its inner and outer functions, our breath being the secret agent, the link between the visible and the invisible.

> For breath is the mysterious, great master who reins unknown and unnamed behind all and everything—who silently commands the function of muscle and joints—who puts the brakes in the rhythmic structure and dictates the phrasing of the flowing passages—who above and beyond all this, regulates the temper of expression in its interplay with the colorfulness of rhythm and melody (Wigman, 1966 p. 11).

Looking back, it is interesting to see what sticks with us—the imprints we have chosen to hang on to, and what we erase over time. What is the reference we make, is it to dance, to relationships, to being a mother, a performer, a teacher, an immigrant?

A native of Germany, I was born at the dawn of the Second World War, growing up in Weimar, part of Soviet occupied Germany, later DDR, during and after the war. The youngest of three children, my mother was a pianist, my father a businessman with ambitions to become a pilot. He was drafted into the war when I was about one. I saw him a few times after that for brief visits, before he was declared missing in action in 1943, in the Battle of Stalingrad. My memory of him is a picture with a black ribbon.

Between age 4 and 6, war, sirens sounding at night. I'm woken up fully dressed.... Take your little suitcase and go into the bomb-shelter, the basement of the house. Oma had to be carried down; she didn't want to go. My sister, Barbara, is standing in the corridor of the bomb shelter, crying. I see the gas masks hanging on the wall, light flickers, dust falls from the ceiling. Someone got hit in the neighborhood, they said.

Why am I always upside down? I stand on my head in the living room, on the big armchair, my mother sort of laughingly acknowledging and embarrassedly excusing me to a visitor. Outside on the swing-set, I hang on the bar and swing holding on by my knees or my feet, wound around the ropes. Or I stand on the board swinging. I hang from the top bar, climb the iron bar up to the top, grabbing and pushing with my feet, higher and higher. I'm being watched with some awe, astonishment. I get attention from family and others sitting in the yard. Monkey-like, I climb trees. I cartwheel through the Goethe Park, as we promenade to the cemetery on weekends. I love to run and cartwheel instead of walking. I always want to run. I don't understand why people are walking instead of running. I practice handstands, headstands, bridges, shoulder stands, cobras, cartwheels, over and over, for hours, outside in the yard on the lawn, by myself.

School is sporadic because of air raids and the scarcity of teachers. My first grade teacher died during an air raid. We are schooled in shifts, 8 a.m. to 1 p.m. and 2 p.m. to 6 p.m. With the pre-alarm of the sirens, we run to the next bomb shelter or try to make it home. I remember running uphill to make it home in time, my mother running towards me to meet me halfway and find a bomb shelter. Sometimes, we go into the "cave," a real cave in the Goethe Park made into a bomb shelter. It is cold and eerie. They talk about the phosphor bomb. It is a new kind, when it hits, the phosphor, a liquid. They say it burns and keeps burning even when you jump into the river. Throughout school, I'm afraid of school. I'm good at hiding. I make myself as invisible as possible.

Between age 7 and 12, after the war—ruins, houses ripped apart, ripped in half with furniture hanging out. You could see parts of kitchens or living rooms, wires, exposed beams, lamps still dangling, a toilet still standing. In my street, we had several such houses. A girlfriend and I venture to go there, along the edge of the field, sneaking through the back. The fence was ripped or down, and we played and found some things that were strewn around the yard. It was exciting.

My aunt Marianne was an opera singer and takes me to the theater when they need children for the opera, theater plays, or ballet. I'm part of a group of kids, all children of theater employees. We meet for rehearsals, participate in performances, and spend much time with opera singers, dancers, and actors in the green room. Sometimes they give us a rehearsal room and we spend time doing yoga, without knowing the term—it's bridges, shoulder stands, headstands, showing each other our favorite moves, as we stay there late into the evening. Sometimes we get some food. We try on make-up, wigs, and costumes. These famous opera singers make jokes and laugh a lot; they like the kids and sometimes we get a hug or ride on someone's knee while we are waiting. It is a joyful bunch of people, a different world. The dancers are in costumes and make-up. To me they are out of this world, so beautiful. I want to be like them. I want to be a dancer. I see them perform, watching from the wings, or while being on stage with them. Women singers and actors who are waiting for their next scene sit around knitting and talking quietly. It is a warm atmosphere. I feel safe here, more than anywhere else. It is an ongoing part of my life, age eight to sixteen.

I had wished to become a dancer and dreamed about it. In a dream, I was "informed" about going to the Palucca School and could audition. This may sound far-fetched, but it was totally real to me. I am grateful to my mother who took my dream seriously and supported my wishes.

Instructed by this dream, I applied to the Palucca School of Dance in Dresden, Germany, one of the two prestigious schools of dance in East Germany at the time. Going through two auditions and a trial period of six months, from hundreds of applicants, I was one of the sixteen remaining. It was a privilege and I felt privileged. Modeled after a Russian ballet school, we lived in dorms, got clothing and a stipend. Our schedule was rigorous, with a daily schedule of ballet, the Waganowa method taught by an elite group of ballet teachers, and modern dance, taught by Gret Palucca. It was there that I learned Palucca was a student of Mary Wigman. After two years of rigid and meticulous studies at this school, I left my country (DDR) to immigrate to West Berlin and continued my studies with Mary Wigman. Dance was my way out.

As a student in 1957 at the Mary Wigman School of Dance, I participated in *Le Sacre du Printemps*, which Wigman choreographed for the Berlin Opera Ballet, and she included some of her students to perform in this work. In addition, during my time of studies, for five years I was part of the dance ensemble for the Beyreuther Festspiele, the renowned Richard Wagner Festival, under the direction of Wieland Wagner and the choreographers Birgit Culberg, Gertrude Wagner, among others. During my time as a student with Mary Wigman, my dance idol was Dore Hoyer. Dore Hoyer was a guest teacher at the Wigman School, a mesmerizing performer and a masterful representative of the Ausdruckstanz, or Expressionist Dance. As a soloist, she was skilled, powerful, and mesmerizing, an authentic choreographer.

During my last years of training at the Wigman School of Dance, I became a bit of an idol myself. I was praised with complements; "You are one in a million." I felt confident and optimistic about my future, totally immersed in the world of dance and music, and rather ignorant of the political climate that I had experienced during my early life in East Germany.

Motion Berlin emerged in 1962. I was a founding member together with Inge Sehnert und Hellmut Gottschild. Motion was well received by the press: "Dance as pure movement phenomenon" (Die Welt); "...ecstasy, yet one to the ultimate etherealized brilliant awareness" (Göttinger Tageblatt); "A new phase of Modern Dance has begun with 'Motion.' ... All traditional conceptions of dance are left off. New scopes of life and experience are approached in dance movement." (Kurier, Berlin. 1964).

When I met Manfred Fischbeck who became my partner, husband, and the father of my daughters, he was not a dancer, but was intrigued by what he saw at Motion Berlin. Manfred and I met on a Motion Berlin tour to Zagreb, Yugoslavia, when he had joined as our tour manager. After our performances, we traveled together to the Croatian island of Hvar. When we met back in Berlin, after the tour, I learned that Manfred was not anymore a stranger to the lifestyle of the West. When we met, I saw him mainly merged in a world of theater and nightlife. I in contrast, was seen only in the circles of dance. He was in one world and I in another. He was a hidden poet, while I was on the esoteric side of dance making, dancing 5–8 hours a day, making my own music, inspired by Musique Concrete, performing, touring, philosophizing about dance, and dreaming dances. For some time, I was a dance favorite, animating a trend in the way I moved, dressed, and cut my hair.

Brigitta Herrmann, solo dance *Ambience*, 1963 (photograph courtesy Motion Berlin).

To me, sharing in his world felt exciting, new and daring. He introduced me to the Beatles, and the Rolling Stones. I was impressed by him; he was impressed by me.

Together we went to see the Living Theater in Berlin. I was stunned by their ruggedness and their almost brutal way of moving. While my world was about abstract, extremely refined dances—solos, duets, and small group forms, here I felt drawn to a form of expression of physical theater and their sense of community. Their political and social activism was fueled by outrage. Their outright protest, their disobedient, blatant actions were mind-boggling, from screaming slogans to taking off their clothes and inviting the audience to do the same.

The Living Theater resided in Berlin at the Akademie der Künste, "Academy of Arts" at the Tiergarten, "Animal Garden," a beautiful and well-tended park during the mid 60s.

Motion Berlin also performed at the Akademie der Künste featured together with the Alvin Ailey American Dance Theater, the Nederlands Dans Theater, and The First Chamber Dance Quartet of New York. Our dances at the time were short abstract compositions, with themes such as *Five Dances in White*, *Haiku*, *Malvena*, and *Stadion*. The context was a paradise of sorts, not that Berlin was without political conflict. The student movements of the left were active and outspoken and the demonstrations occurred not without violence. Demonstrations were frequent and in part caused by the assassination attempt on Rudi Dutschke. Rudi Dutschke was the most prominent spokesperson of the German student movement who advocated a "long March through the Institutions," opting for a peaceful revolution. He survived this assassination attempt for another 12 years, and died at the age of 39 due to his injuries. A street near this location now carries his name. I remember the day when this shooting occurred. I happened to walk by at the location prior to when he was shot. I knew Rudi; he was friends with one of my college mates who shared an apartment with other students. It was a huge and shocking event for all of us.

Moreover, the Tiergarten was a rather peaceful location. And, while occupied with those 30 some members of the Living Theater the smell of marijuana permeated the air. Those men and women with rugged clothing, long hair, and unusual casual behavior drew much attention. From my rather esoteric, metaphysical understanding and practice of dance, their performance of *Paradise Now* was mind boggling to me. Their use of game-like structures in performance, their spontaneous, ruff and tough interaction with a sense of vigorous dedication, their confidence with an in the moment sense of embodiment, rather than the rehearsed acting of dramatic gestures in conventional theater captivated me.

I believe what was most intriguing to me at the time was their sense of community, a promise of life and work being intrinsically connected.

It turned out those elements of the Living Theater were of shared interest between Manfred and myself as we had witnessed the performance of "Paradise Now" together.

It was a turning point in our relationship. After we observed the Living Theater together, our shared enthusiasm laid the seeds to adopting a new possibility of creating: the ability to create collectively. It was part of the zeitgeist, the idea of communal living, joint creation, and collaboration. Joint everything was "in the air." For us, it became a promise. Creativity sparked by Eros brought us together. With our three personalities and talents, Hellmut Gottschild, Manfred, and myself engaged in a first collaboration entitled *Countdown for Orpheus*. This was a first merging of choreography and structured improvisation in performance. Together with original music, and film, it was the first multimedia production, presented at the Akademie der Kunste in Berlin, in 1967.

Group Motion Company performance of *Countdown for Orpheus* at Jacob's Pillow Dance Festival, from left to right: Barbara Lember, Leny Sloen, Manfred Fischbeck, Brigitta Herrmann, and Hellmut Gottschild, 1969 (photograph courtesy Group Motion).

At the outset of my career, my understanding of dance performance was strictly rooted in choreography as the art of performance, yet sourced through a process of improvisation. It was Mary Wigman's well-deserved merit and method of teaching choreography, originated and fueled by a process of improvisation and meticulously crafted to arrive at a choreographed work of art.

I felt rooted and confirmed by success, having assimilated certain values and the ability to experience myself as a dancer, choreographer and teacher of dance, with the dream of a career as a dancer/choreographer oriented in elusive, esoteric brilliance. When offered the opportunity to join Hellmut and Manfred in the U.S., I had to ask myself, was I was about to leave, give it up, let go of a professional career, a direction as a dancer and choreographer that I had tirelessly pursued and was fixated on, for over ten years?

When I arrived in the U.S. in 1968, I only knew one phrase of English: "How High the Moon," which I'd learned from a popular song in an American dancer's choreography, while participating in her piece at the American House in Berlin. At the time, I told myself, it's okay if I don't speak. I am a dancer; I'll express myself by dancing and demonstrate by using gestures. Asking others, especially my husband, to speak for me became a disabling pattern in my relationship with others. Sitting in with discussions sharpened my skills of observation of body language, and eventually, I absorbed the English language without any formal training.

In 1968, after our arrival in the U.S., Hellmut and I auditioned for Al Carmines, the director of Judson Church Dance Theater, with a repertoire of original solo and duet works. It opened the door to perform there. Manfred joined us soon after, and together with local dancers we reconstructed and performed *Countdown for Orpheus*. Other opportunities to perform followed, including an invitation to the Jacob's Pillow Dance Festival. It led to establishing the company in the U.S. as the Group Motion Multimedia Dance Theater. After four years of highly successful collaborative multimedia productions, internal conflict arose from differences in personal values and esthetics. Hellmut left the Group Motion Multimedia Dance Theater to form his company, Zero Moving Company, in 1972. With Manfred and I left to share direction of the company, our personal and professional relationship evolved along with concepts of dance performance, teaching of dance, and building a family.

Several unrelated sources contributed to the emergence of the original Group Motion Workshop: the foundation of dance as it was transmitted through Mary Wigman's teaching, her references to the mystic and the invisible forces of life, the experience of the Living Theater with its dimensions of physical and communal creation, and our experience with the Divine Light Mission (Divya Sandesh Parishad, DLM), a vital community at the time, and a lead-in to practice of meditation and to Eastern philosophy and Buddhism. It did not occur out of thin air. Our experience of the counter culture of the 60s also included experimentation with hallucinogens, and these mind-altering practices and experimentations all contributed to a time of self-exploration and social change.

Additionally, the Group Motion Workshop grew out of working with a company of professional and non-professional dancers. Group Motion games and structures evolved and served to generate movement and choreographic seeds and patterns. When including people untrained in dance technique, the Group Motion Company's performance style grew to a synthesis of both choreography and improvisation based on the game structures. Structures were needed to provide form, inspire creativity, and assist orientation in space and time in the context of performance. They attested to stimulate creativity, maintain vitality and sustainability. Performances were recreated anew each time as they were performed, and entranced performers and their audiences in new ways, sourcing unseen motifs, and serving as building blocks of dance vocabulary. Shifting towards improvisation, the structures stimulated movement patterns and communication, the spontaneous creation of images, and of forms generated from the inside out. This became the new skill—a skill driven by sensibility and listening, and by tuning into heightened awareness, supported by counterculture, and by the consciousness-raising trend of spiritual movements coming from the East to the West.

It was around 1970 when some friends told us about an opportunity of a downtown space, an empty three-story clothing store for rent as a studio and a space to live—The Al Berman store. The old Al Berman Clothing Store, still with clothes racks and even some leftover sweaters still hanging left behind, and I happened to wear them for years to come. The clothing store was on the corner of 5th and South Streets in Philadelphia, a three story building which we rented when all the merchants had moved out of the area. They had moved out of concern for the anticipated Highway ramp that was to be built along the South Street border. As the area became deserted by the business community it declined in value, and with rents way down it drew in the artists, Hippies and crafts people, who made their shops, cafe's, and studios. Eventually, as the protests against the ramp succeeded, the South street area became one of the most thriving, colorful neighborhoods, the "Village" of Philadelphia.

We had moved from our first studio, an old Firehouse in Roxborough, to 5th and South Street, inhabiting this building. It provided us with a studio space on the first floor and the two floors above became shared living spaces. We lived there, approximately eight people on the 2nd floor and four people on the 3rd floor. It made our rent payment affordable as we shared the space with fellow dancers, filmmakers, and musicians and it offered a space for intense collaborative creation amongst the artistic entities. It was during this time, in 1971, that the Group Motion Workshop originated. A very specific sequence of instructions was channeled through me as I was holding the microphone and serving as the instructor. Later known as the programation, it became the blueprint for the Group Motion Friday Night Workshop. Each workshop began with this programation, which has been impregnated into my memory. The sequence of programs given to the participants led them from a meditative state into stretching, into various kinds of traveling, falling, rolling, shaking, and activating body parts. It was a warm up in preparation for play and movement communication, starting with a meditation.

Sit and cross your legs in front of you:
Focus on your breathing...
Breathe deeply and evenly throughout your whole body...
Feel the expansion and contraction as you in- and exhale...
Feel your breath like a wave moving through your body...

It felt magical at the time and still does. The dance ended in slow motion, people holding hands weaving together through the space.

It was in its inception a channeled event that felt like magic. And, it was shorty after the initiation into meditation that several members of the Group Motion Company got initiated and drawn into this spiritual practice, called Knowledge, offered through the Divine Light Mission. Friends of ours approached us with the request to provide space for 200 Canadians, who came by bus to Philadelphia to receive Knowledge. The term to receive "Knowledge" was used to describe the initiation into this spiritual practice. When we complied with our friends' request to house those 200 Canadians, they slept in the studio, packed in like sardines in a can. This was followed with a next request of providing the space for knowledge initiation. As we complied, miraculously within 24 hours the entire building was transformed into a domain where Indian Mahatmas in long gowns, dozens of "premies" and knowledge seekers occupied our space, sitting in lotus positions or on their knees listening to Satsang or meditating quietly by hovering under a sheet. It was peculiar and mystifying to observe, so, that I felt drawn into, and moved to heed the opportunity to "receive knowledge" as well. In doing so, I and other Group Motion members became part of a movement that led to following and adhering to a practice of meditation.

During the next six or seven years we carried on, more or less loosely following and even traveling to some of their events, including to Montreal, Florida and to Rome in Italy. Traveling to Rome in 1982, I recall this was our last journey in following. Meanwhile we were a family of four, our daughters born in 1974 and 1976.

My first daughter was born in the spring of 1974. When I became pregnant, I felt exhilarated and monitored the internal and external changes of my body and mind. I had no preconceived ideas of pregnancy or birthing, no fear, just the joy of feeling the sensations of a growing life inside of me, and the anticipation of a child. I conducted the Friday Night Workshop the night before labor started, and went easily through the next day with contractions. By Saturday evening we decided to check into the hospital.

I remember my feeling of dislike when entering the hospital. A nurse with a bored demeanor demanded various routine procedures that I rigorously refused. I did not want any interference with my breathing and wanted to focus on the rising and receding waves. The baby was born early on the Sunday of Mother's Day. I remember the joy when my baby was held up to me and we made eye contact. There was the sense of recognition and a tender smile. Twenty month after Laina's arrival, Aura was born. This time at home with a midwife present. Both the processes of pregnancy and of giving birth were empowering and life-altering for me.

From 1976 until 1982, we lived on a farm near Morgantown, PA, sharing the property with two other families. We occupied the big farmhouse, while one of the other houses was occupied by a family, also with two children, and the third house occupied by a woman with one child. All of the children were around the same age. The farmhouses were surrounded by abundance of land some of which was still occupied by the owner to keep horses. We had use of much of the land, a huge barn and a beautiful pond. Those years appeared as a kind of paradise, filled with gatherings of friends, and seekers of sorts, coming together on the farm to play music and dance.

Living in the countryside, we experimented with dance and music improvisation and continuing with meditation and a simple lifestyle. The freedom of living close to nature offered a sense of peace and liberty to ourselves and our children. It felt like a prosperous life style, yet without a lot of money, but with abundance, an abundance of friends and sharing of creativity and family life. As I recall the events of this time, I believe that much of the desire to be part of a community of trust and peace, of hope and support gave rise to following the larger, tremendous movement of tens of thousands of people, following and practicing in hope of a more real, more truthful and fulfilled lifestyle, away from commercialism, away from racism, away from the tensions of competition and fear. People from all religious traditions and ethnic backgrounds breaking away from their dead-end dogmatic rigid traditions were looking to find something new, something to share and agree on and something related to the zeitgeist. Most of us had experimented with drugs one way or another; marijuana, hashish, LSD, Mescaline were part of my own experience and explorations before I had children. Not on an ongoing daily basis but occasionally. It was widely used and offered among musicians and other artists and it offered and induced insightful knowledge and stimulated mind-expanding events, never-ending adventures of consciousness expanding perceptions, visions and illuminations in combination with dance, and with music playing, collective creation in performances and other participatory happenings.

While raising my two children, commuting from the countryside to teach at the Philadelphia College of Performing Arts, now the University of the Arts, and the University of Pennsylvania, I taught in addition to performing, choreographing, and touring with the Group Motion company, and then implemented a Group Motion children's dance program. My life was very full and I was moving towards burnout. This coincided with my divorce and led to a profound experience of transformation and restructuring of my life's direction. I immersed myself in the research and practices of spirituality and holistic health, including: Body Mind Centering, Live Arts Process, Kinetic Awareness, Reiki, Hands of Light, Sound Healing, and Reflexology, in continuation with practices of yoga and meditation.

For the next several years, I continued the executive and artistic co-directorship of Group Motion. Yet, my interest shifted again towards my Mary Wigman dance roots when I met and joined with Michael A. Carson in founding and directing Ausdruckstanz Dance Theater (ADT). With ADT, a company rooted in principals and philosophy of Mary Wigman and inspired by the work of Pina Bausch, I refocused my skills of performance and choreography. In this context, my work was featured on public television, toured in colleges, theaters, and festivals, locally, regionally, and internationally. We opened our studio The Dance Workspace in the

Fishtown area of Philadelphia with an exhibit about The Life and Work of Mary Wigman.

The Dance Workspace was lost to an electrical fire in 1996, together with the loss of twenty-eight years of personal and professional belongings. For about a year, I was homeless, oscillating between Philadelphia and visiting my mother in Germany. My mother passed on in the same year, at the age of 90. It was during this time that my interest in dance as a form of therapy grew and led me to pursue a Masters of Art at Naropa University in Boulder, Colorado.

When I entered Naropa University in 1999, in this new environment, away from my routine and duties of Ausdruckstanz Dance Theater in Philadelphia, I felt revitalized. Influenced by somatic studies and practices of observation as they were taught at Naropa University, I searched for what was next in my performance work. The ambition of "meeting the moment," the practice of meditation was central to the Naropa experience, and was already a trend and appeared as the new direction, as a way of life. When the opportunity for performance offered itself, I experimented with solo improvisation in performance. Using minimal scores to time myself, yet otherwise nothing made-up, trusting to follow the impulses of the moment including percussion and vocalization.

After four years of studies and teaching at Naropa University, I returned to Philadelphia. Since then, my performances and workshops continued to explore new territory and collaborations with themes of social change, with personal and global issues and weaving those experiences and ideas into the fabric of teaching Group Motion. My thesis, "Dancing the Present Moment: An Approach to Dance/Movement Therapy based on Group Motion" aimed to summarize those new insights. Excerpts of this work have been woven into the narrative of this book.

Group Motion has evolved and was sustained through stages of change for fifty years now. While the company's profile has shifted, changed its leadership and focus, the Group Motion Workshop has sustained and evolved as a practice. It is a story of improvisation directed by vision and spiritual practice, our two realities manifesting into one, evolving over time, with the participation of thousands.

Running into Dance: Manfred's Story

Throughout the early part of my life, I was running—running away, or running towards or running just to run. At a kindergarten fire when I was three years old, I was told that I tried to run into the fire but someone pulled me back. Later, in my teens I was running in the woods playing outdoor games with my friends, always being the last one to stop playing, still running when everyone else had stopped. Years later in the streets of West Berlin, I ran from water-throwing police during anti war demonstrations of student revolution, and then, one day, I ran into a form of movement called Dance that I had never seen before, and that would change my life.

I was born in Africa during World War II, and spent three years of my life there with my mother and older brother. We lived in internment camps that the British army had set up for all the Germans they imprisoned from the German controlled territory, "Tanganyika," later to become Tanzania. All men, including my father had been separated from their families and sent to a different camp in South Africa. I was told that one of the favorite activities of my brother and I was to run along side of the fence of the camp, the outside of which we called "Inside" for some strange reason. After three years of internment camp, we were allowed to return to Germany in exchange for the release of Jewish prisoners from a concentration camp in Germany. The journey took almost a year, including a boat ride on a British troupe transporter up the Indian Ocean, another eight-month-long stay in a camp in Palestine, and then a lengthy train ride through the Balkans and Austria. We finally arrived in a small town in Northern Germany called Stendal at the end of the war, coming into the thick of things with bombs falling and houses burning and refugees in flight and tanks of foreign armies rolling in. After the war, this town and the surrounding area fell under Russian occupation and became Communist East Germany, later the DDR. Here I spent nine years of my childhood and early adolescence, going to school, learning to play violin and piano, singing in a church choir, and passionately playing soccer and other outdoor sports and games. There was no dance to be found in this town. The only dance experience I recall took place sometime around age five in a nearby village. There was a Sunday afternoon children's dance event at the inn of one of my uncles. All children of the village were put into a circle and had to walk around to music, what kind I do not recall. My brother and I resisted this procedure and hid under a table, but someone pulled us out by our hair and made us join the circle.

While there was no dance, there was a lot of music in my life—violin and piano practice and singing Bach in a choir in the beautiful gothic churches in town. I must have been eight, and my father caught me improvising on the piano and sarcastically commented, "Oh, here goes little

Beethoven." There was a lot of movement in my life in the form of soccer playing; I dreamt up soccer moves before falling asleep at night. I ran in the parks and nearby forests as part of outdoor game playing with my friends, and enjoyed acting out stories in front of my class at school, before the teacher came in.

In looking back, I believe that my obsession with playing and performing movement activities in tandem with my intensive music practice provided the seeds for my dance/music calling. All in all, I remember having been pretty happy in spite of all the hardships of those years. Throughout the end of the war, and after the war time, people did not have enough to eat, and fathers and uncles were lost or dead, or had been taken prisoners of war in far away lands. That included my own father who was kept prisoner of war in Africa and did not return until I was 7 years old. When the heavily destroyed towns and cities were still in ruins, no one spoke about what had happened. No one gave us any explanations. There was a big silence about it. And the war mysteries and the silence about them provided a strange and hard to fathom subtext to my growing up, that I was only becoming aware of many years later.

At age 14, I left Stendal and East Germany, The German Democratic Republic, for West Berlin, because I was not permitted to go to High School for political reasons. My father was a religion teacher. I never joined the Communist youth organization called, "Young Pioneers." In fact, I had some classmates defect and join the Christian youth organization called "Jungschar" (Young Bunch or Young Tribe). I was declared an "Enemy of the State" at age 14.

My parents decided to take me to West Berlin, where my older sister already had escaped with her husband, and where every day thousands of other East German rejected school kids like me were seeking refuge. My mother took me there on a train and dropped me off at a boarding school for East German student refugees, and then she went back to Stendal. This was, of course, before the wall.

I went to high school and later, the University in West Berlin, living in boarding homes until I was old enough to live on my own. Still, there was no dance in my life, other than some free form party dancing to New Orleans jazz. I studied literature and began to write poetry and practiced music, only to the extent that I played the old upright piano in our boarding home, and later in bars during drinking trips with my friends. I had picked up some American tunes, "Rock Around the Clock" and "Moonlight Serenade" and began to improvise the Boogie-woogie.

At the University, I became part of a theater troupe. One of the

Manfred Fischbeck in *Soundscapes* at Cafe Einstein, Berlin, 1980 (photograph courtesy Group Motion).

actresses in this troupe actually was a dancer and invited me one day to come to her dance school, to help her with some music for a solo dance that she was working on. So I stepped into the Mary Wigman School of Dance, having never heard of it before, and this day became, without my knowing it, a turning point. I saw dance, modern dance that is, for the first time. I saw Mary Wigman teach from a chair. She was already in her late seventies, not knowing that she was one of the pioneers of modern dance and world-renowned. I was invited by my friend Inge to watch them practice their dances that they were preparing for a concert, the first one for their group called "Motion Berlin."

It was a group of three, two women and one man, Brigitta Herrmann, Katharina Sehnert, and Hellmut Gottschild. They were creating rather short, abstract, highly intricate and refined dances to mostly avant-garde or electronic music. It was all new to me, but I was attracted by what I saw and heard. It was during one piece called *Stadion* that I remember being particularly affected by one movement performed by one of the dancers, Brigitta Herrmann. This movement, a slow and deep contraction, as well as other movements and images in Brigitta's dances created a space that was sensuous and abstract, mystical and yet of luminous clarity. Something was moved inside me. At the time, I had no idea where this experience would take me.

I continued to live rebelliously within my communal family of friends and artists, engaging in making theater, film, writing literature papers and poetry. My consciousness of the communal life in the ghetto city of West Berlin was intensely inspired and expanded by a book that my brother had given to me. *The Diary of Justyna* was written by a young Jewish woman in the Krakow ghetto and told the story of her and her friends, a group of resistance fighters living in a house in the ghetto, fighting their hopeless but highly committed fight not just for survival, but for their own dignity and pride. This book had become my guiding light.

I was beginning to build a career as an actor without serious intention. The theater group from the university evolved into an independent professional theater group called "Provisorisches Theater," under the direction of and in partnership with my friend Ruediger Tuchel. We had some major and somewhat groundbreaking successes with innovative staging of *The Good God of Manhattan*, by Ingeborg Bachmann, *Orphee* by Jean Cocteau, and *In the Jungle of the City* by Bertolt Brecht. We had substantial support from the city of Berlin. I was acting (without any acting training) while pursuing literature studies and writing poetry. I had written a paper on Paul Celan's poem "Sprachgitter," a poem that spoke the impossibility of speaking the unspeakable. My teacher, Peter Scondi, arranged for me to meet Paul Celan, a Jewish poet from Rumania, who had barely escaped the Holocaust. Celan was living in Paris, writing in the German language. His most famous poem "Todesfuge" (Death Fugue) was the first poem ever written about the Holocaust. My meeting with him lasted only an hour, but moved me profoundly. The challenge of writing poetry in this language that was corrupted by the German culture of the recent past was a duality that I was painfully experiencing in my own writing process. Meeting Celan, and experiencing the depth of his writing that seemed to be on the way to silence, moved me further in my search for other forms of expression.

Meanwhile, I was keeping in contact with the dance of "Gruppe Motion," our informal name for Motion Berlin, and I took up some studies in mime with one of the teachers at the Wigman studio. One summer, Motion Berlin was invited to perform at the music festival in Zagreb, Yugoslavia. I accompanied the group as a stage manager on this trip. At the end of the festival, during a short vacation week on the island of Hvar, I got to know and become personally close with Brigitta. Being of opposing nature on many levels, we were attracted to each other in many ways that we did not fully understand at the time.

Shortly after our return from Yugoslavia, Brigitta and I went to see *Mysteries*, and *Paradise Now*, improvisational movement theater performance on the stage of the Academie der Kuenste. It was The Living Theater, the truly revolutionary troupe from New York under the direction of Julian Beck and Judith Malina. This was the second pivotal experience that would move me towards dance and movement. There was one piece in particular in this performance that had a special impact on me, and gave me the experience and realization that movement is a language, a most powerful language of expression and communication that everyone can speak and understand.

This Living Theater "game" or structure was a ritual of movement creation and sharing that was simple and powerful; it was both dance and theater that everyone could grasp. (For a version of the structure, see the Exchange Game.) Having been engaged in poetry writing and thinking, acting and making theater, studying literature and history, and taking part in the student revolution, I had been feeling dissatisfied, lost and despairing. Here, I was turned around and saw possibilities for a different life. I saw the power of the communal/collective creativity of the Living Theater. The revolutionary dimension of a non-violent, non-antagonizing, compassionate and peaceful language, the language of dance and movement as a liberating human potential began to dawn on me.

It was around the same time that Motion Berlin had begun to create a large and ambitious project, a multimedia dance theater work, probably the first one of its kind in Germany. It was city funded, and I was asked to join the project as a collaborator in concept development, text writer, filmmaker, and dramaturge. It was my first engagement in the context of dance. I was still not dancing myself. Seven dancers including Brigitta Herrmann and Hellmut Gottschild performed the piece, *Countdown for Orpheus*. Thomas Kessler created the live percussive and taped electronic music. I provided texts and film images. The piece was based on the Orpheus myth, interpreted as a shift from individual to collective consciousness of creation, combining the framing concepts of sleep and dream on one hand, and a count down for a spaceship start on the other. It was highly layered, featuring new concepts of choreography, music, and multimedia presentation. It had mixed reviews and audience responses.

Kathy Pira, one of the dancers in the group, an American from Philadelphia, invited us to come visit her in the States to check out the dance scene. She thought the work would go over well there. We accepted

Count Down for Orpheus performance at Jacob's Pillow Dance Festival, from left to right: Kathy Pira, Manfred Fischbeck and Vickie Seitchik, 1969 (photograph courtesy Group Motion).

the invitation, and one and a half years later, this piece initiated Group Motion's American existence. These performances would mark my dancing debut, at Temple University in Philadelphia and at Judson Church in New York, with the company of seven dancers that Group Motion had gathered in Philadelphia. But prior to all this, back in Berlin, I had applied and had just been accepted as a student of the Film Akademie Berlin. I had made my first debut in a major role in a movie by Volker Schloendorff, *Mord und Totschlag, A Degree in Murder*, and played my first major role in a state theater of Berlin in *Saved* by Edward Bond, directed by Peter Zadek. In both roles, I played a dropout, a somewhat asocial teenager with no aim or goal other than surviving. Ironically, I had just found my own goal and a new direction to dance with Group Motion in America, and these film and theater projects actually made the money that I needed to follow it. The pull towards dance and multimedia theater and their revolutionary and transformational potential was so strong, I felt it in my body; it overrode all of the other options, in spite of their career opportunities.

All of this took place against the backdrop of the intense student revolution movement in West Berlin, that pretty much all of my friends and the people of my generation were actively engaged in. We had been running and marching in the city's streets or crowding in sit-ins at the universities, protesting the cover up of war and after war traumas, the senseless status quo of a divided city, a divided country, a divided world, rallying for change and a new political and social order. This protest and rally, however undefined or unclear it seemed at times was summed up with the coded term "The Long March of the Revolution," a term that spanned from the Cultural Revolution of China, to all the student revolutions of Europe and America, and to the Che Guevara campaigns in the jungles of South America.

One summer night, I was introduced by a friend to someone in a bar; this someone was Andreas Bader, who later was to become one of the leaders of the radical leftist Bader Meinhoff Group. I was introduced to him with the words, "This is Manfred and he is about to go to America to dance." I knew this would sound to him as an escapist, if not counter revolutionary plan. America and dance? I received a sarcastic smile on Bader's face. In my mind, without saying it out loud, I repeated the mantra that I had recently created for myself. " I rather dance than march in the streets." For me, at this moment the mantra stood its ground. About three years later, I read in an American newspaper that he and his group had begun to wage a terrorist war, which would last many years, and eventually ended in a German high security prison. The "Long March" of the revolution for me was about to take a different turn.

In the summer of 1968, I followed Brigitta Herrmann and Hellmut Gottschild to America with practically nothing, other than my desire to work with Hellmut and Brigitta on the creation of a new existence and the making of multimedia dance theater work. Brigitta had also become my partner in life, and I then started to train in dance. My life long running, from running along the fences in the internment camps, to running in the woods and soccer fields of the after war teenage years, to running in the streets of West Berlin dreaming of revolution, my running had turned into dance.

For two years after our American debut, the three Germans from Berlin continued working together on the creation of dance theater works, one of which was the highly successful piece based on Kafka's novel *Amerika* and in particular on the last chapter of the book, *The Great Theater of Oklahoma Is Calling You*. After that, Hellmut Gottschild decided to leave the Company and form his own as Zero Moving Company. Brigitta and I had gotten married and continued on as co-directors and moved the Company to 5th and South Streets in Philadelphia. Here, we continued to practice and develop improvisational dance/movement structures and games and to create multimedia dance performances. It was also here that we connected to the meditation practice of the Divine Light Mission and Guru Maharaji, when we were asked by a friend if the studio could be used for "knowledge sessions" for a weekend.

It was in this context of playing music for dance that I re-discovered my interest in music playing, taking a course on electronic music with a Moog synthesizer at the Philadelphia College of Art (now The University of the Arts), and subsequently obtaining an instrument similar to the Mini Moog, an ElectroComp 100. The combination of melodic, harmonic, rhythmic and textural sound, instantly interchangeable on the same instrument, turned out to be perfect for the practice of improvisational music playing with improvisational dance.

It was this power of dance music interaction in a spontaneous happening that pulled people off the street into our studio on South Street one summer night in 1971. The company of 15 who was communally sharing their living quarters in the upper floors of the former Al Berman's Clothing store was practicing in the first floor studio. Feeling permission by the zeitgeist of the time, and the particular South Street village energy, people walked in and some of them joined in the guided improvisation that Brigitta was spontaneously inspired to lead while I was playing music. This overlap of company and non-professional dancers dancing together, in a guided improvisation with live music, was the spark for the creation of the Group Motion Workshop format that continues every Friday Night.

Meanwhile, the company moved again to a new place on 4th and South into a larger two-story studio space. It was there that we had our first daughter Laina, with Aura the second one to follow two years later. Having the two young children motivated us to move to the country for a few years. While the work of teaching at the University of Pennsylvania and the College of Performing Arts in Philadelphia continued, an hour and a half drive into the city was a daily challenge. But the beautiful natural environment of the farm was the balancing aspect of our life. It was there that the practice of meditation expanded the consciousness of living and working in a powerful way, also bringing me back to a new empowerment of writing poetry. Along with the nature experience, we also had the fortune to live in community with friends and their children.

Prior to our move to the country in 1973, Group Motion was invited to join the National Endowment Touring Program and the Company soon began to tour nationally and internationally, bringing our performance work and the workshop structures to many different places and environments. One of those early tours took Brigitta and me to Antioch College, and it was there that we met Elia Sinaiko and that the writing of this book was initiated. In a four-week intensive session at Elia's house on Cape Cod, the three of us churned out the basic concept of a book about the Group Motion approach to dance improvisation. We did not know that it would take over forty years to come to the point of finally completing it.

Throughout this time, the work continued to grow and pass through many processes of being tested and expanded, in application to teaching, creation, or performance practice. In 1988, Brigitta and I divorced, but continued to work together as co-directors of Group Motion until 1989 when she co-founded a new company, Ausdruckstanz Dance Theater. We continue to co-direct the Group Motion Workshop in Philadelphia and in retreats today.

As a faculty member at the dance department at the University of the Arts, and as a choreographer and director in the context the Group Motion Dance Company, I had many opportunities for collaborative exchanges with other national and international artists. Butoh dancer Masaki Iwana from Tokyo/Paris, London New Zealand choreographer Carol Brown, Argentinian choreographer Oscar Araiz, Philadelphia Hip Hop dancer and choreographer Rennie Harris, Japanese choreographer Akiko Kitamura, and many others— through these connections the Company and I were invited to tour and to share the Group Motion work.

The Company received generous funding and the opportunity to create a body of multimedia dance theater works in collaborative creation, and through that engage with and nourish many dancers of the Philadelphia dance community. From 1998 until 2002, under Group Motion's leadership, we formed an artist driven cooperative of several dance companies including Rennie Harris Pure Movement, Scrap Performance Group, and Ausdruckstanz under the name of Kumquat Dance Center, and operated out of the Community Education Center in West Philadelphia.

Throughout all this same time, the Group Motion Friday Night Workshop as well as Group Motion Workshop Retreats continued to go on and thrive, evolve, and even expand into satellite workshops held at other places.

This book and the game structures within it were born from a labor of shared love, mutual inspiration, and commitment to dance/movement improvisation and its liberating, healing and transformational power. Over almost 50 years, Brigitta Herrmann and I continued to build it together, even through times of being apart and working in separate places and with different focuses. As the "Long March" of Group Motion is still going, we are finally putting the mark of this book down on our shared personal path, hopefully contributing to the global journey of contemporary dance. At its heart, it harbors the knowing that dance and movement, and all art forms, are vital languages of expression, communication and transformation for all people, carrying a revolutionary potential for the planet and its desperate need for peace. Thanks to all who joined this journey in the past and who are moving/dancing it with us in the present and into the future.

Group Motion Performance Stories

From a spontaneous performance in the Glasgow Airport to a ruin in Berlin, here are some examples of the more dramatic contexts of Group Motion game structures in action. These stories describe a range of experiences with professionals and those new to dance.

The Glasgow Airport

At the Glasgow Airport waiting room, the plane to New York is five hours late—five hours of waiting and sitting and the usual boredom. Suddenly, we see a young man moving in slow motion, twisting, turning and rolling towards the center of the room. We wonder who this is and if he isn't a little strange. Then, we see that there are three more people moving center-ward from the corners of the room. When they meet, a dance evolves—touching, holding, and reflecting each other's movements in a group improvisation. On return from a performance in Berlin, the Group Motion Multimedia Dance Company has transformed the airport space. This was before flash mobs, before the Internet.

So we are in this airport for five hours, and waiting and sitting and bored to death. And I mentioned something about how we should start playing a game, some kind of game. And we went to the four corners of the room. We went to the four corners of the space, and before we left we said, "We'll meet you. We'll meet here in the middle." And we all took our time going to the center, walking on tables, going over chairs.

In slow motion.

Rolling next to people.

And the thing that happened though—you could feel the people. I had to completely not look at anyone, ignore them.

We built this space around us and started playing the Active-Passive game with each other. We sat ... we did very natural things, sat each other down in chairs and crossed the legs, moved around and closed eyes and other stuff. And none of that was planned. We just planned to come to the center.

When it was all over, almost everyone stood up and ran over. They started writing down numbers and all kinds of things.

It was like all of a sudden, it was over, and thirty people just WHOOSH!

Making *Inroads*—Berlin

In 1996, The Group Motion Dance Company was in residence at the "Tacheles," an arts center in the heart of Berlin "Mitte," the middle of the city, located in a grand building, partially still a ruin from World War II. The piece we were presenting was called *Inroads*, but before the performance, we started an improvisational dance on the very busy street in front of the theater. We engaged in some sort of flocking dance in varying formations. We stopped the trolley cars on both sides of the street. For about five minutes, they played along and stayed still, but then they started slowly to move in on the dancers, at which point the dancers quickly moved into the theater. A good number of people who had watched, spontaneously followed them, even if they had not intended to see the performance. We had made "inroads" into a certain space for the dance in the public arena, with the spontaneous engagement of people on the street. It occurred to us that on that street about forty years earlier, in 1953, the East Berliner workers were marching in protest against the communist regime, and another fifteen years earlier to that, the boots of thousands of Nazi Germany's soldiers had pounded that street. We had come to dance, rather than march, and for a moment, even the uniformed trolley car conductors respected that.

Arche Nova—Pennsylvania

In the Zellerbach Theater in Philadelphia and UPenn in 1973, when at the end of the performance of *Arche Nova*, a multimedia dance theater journey into "outer and inner space," we had the whole theater, including the audience space, serve as a space ship, a new ark. At the end of which, the audience was asked to exit the theater in slow motion, along with the dancers who descended from the stage space. The audience members followed the cue, creating an exodus of grand proportions. Picture that, an entire audience exiting in slow motion.

Massive Flocking—Tokyo

In 1996, Group Motion Dance Company was in residence in Tokyo, Japan, at an International Dance Festival. We are there performing our own multimedia dance work *Cultures*, and "Directions of Harmonization," a piece for the company by Japanese choreographer Kenshi Nohmi.

As part of the residence, we are invited to conduct a workshop at a college with students of gymnastics. When we get there, we find 100 of them waiting for us in a huge gym. After a warm up conducted in groups by three different company members, we decide to work on improvisational structures and the dance/movement games with them. They are very eager and focused. To do "Flocking" in a Triangle format was an obvious choice.

So then there are 30 or so groups of three moving though space and through each other in different speeds, in different directions and levels, including a vertical one, as some of the group climb the walls with built ladders—gymnasts that they are. It is an amazing spectacle of organized multiplicity, of ordered and cooperative chaos, where the balance of the creativity initiated and led by the individual at the tip of the triangle, and the focus of the following group, is the key, the glue that organizes this massive, spontaneously created dance, that most likely had never been seen before in these proportions.

You Changed My Life—Love Park, Philadelphia

The Group Motion Company is performing the last segment of *City Dances*, a site-specific tour through public art sites on the Parkway in 2012. The ten dancers are performing an improvised structure called "Mandala," where three circle rings of different movement phrases are creating a large mandala-like structure in front of the iconic Love sculpture, with its four letters L-O and V-E

Breaking up the circles, they proceed with individual and partnering dances that move them towards the sculpture, and end in a group tableau, inside the letters. The music for the dance comes from iPods and speakers that the dancers wear on their bodies. We had been watching the dance and carrying a large boom box to help amplify the music. A young 10 year-old African American boy had been standing next to me and seemed very excited. At the end of the dance, he ran over to the dancers and hugged them. Later they told me that he said to them, "You changed my life."

Part I.

Group Motion
Game Structures

Solo/Duet

I am
I am delighted
I surprise myself—because
Because I never know what will actually show up

If I have music
The music gives me clues
It triggers my bones, my muscles, and my nerves where I feel
In dance
Feeling is an organ that I rely on
I feed on
Tied in with my breathing
It connects me with You
The person across the room

—Brigitta

Active-Passive

For any number of participants.
With or without music.

The Active-Passive game is an exercise of empathy and compassion. The setup is simple. The objective is nonverbal kinesthetic communication, learning about empathy and trust, sensing comfort or discomfort. It is a form of partnering that uses and plays with all aspects of interaction, from holding, to lifting, to learning how to move a person by asserting caring, comforting ways of touch, including forms of healing touch. The Active-Passive dance requires a sense of tuning in with the other person who has her eyes closed. We create shapes; we indicate traveling or holding a gesture by the way we touch. We generate a sense of expression, by sculpting the body, guiding each other into the space: holding, supporting, sometimes lifting, pulling or gently pushing, tapping, or massaging.

Originally, the Active-Passive structure was generated in the context

Active Passive Dance with Laura Bertin in front of Nicole Levin, Friday Night Workshop, 2015 (photograph courtesy Bill Hebert).

of a performance piece, as a form of interaction between the dancers to create a specific scene. The idea was to establish a contact that was spontaneous and true to the moment and ability of the dancers. In the process, it turned out to become the most popular of structures.

- Participants choose a partner; one person will be active and the other will be passive.
- They will be moving each other through touch.
- Those who are passive stand still and close their eyes.
- Those who are active start to move their passive partner, careful to ensure their partner does not lose balance.
- Like a sculptor, the active person uses touch to move the arms, hands, legs, feet, head, and torso of the passive partner, molding them into different forms and shapes. The active person makes it understood by the way they hold and touch the passive person, that they want the position to be held or released. The active person uses not only hands, but also their body to move the passive partner. The passive partner can also be moved across the floor.

- The passive partner must trust, and be attentive to the direction the active partner is giving with the nature of their touch. The passive partner keeps their eyes closed.

Active-Passive Group Variation

- Several passive people can be joined into larger forms, or several who are active can join together to move one passive person.
- People can change partners, and can change their role of active or passive by opening or closing their eyes.

Active-Passive Zero Gravity

- Upon receiving an impulse from the active partner, the passive partner slowly continues the movement in a non-gravitational flow, until the next impulse is given. The touch impulses should be given in such a way as to keep the passive dancer in a weightless flow of movement.

Active-Passive Body Part Variation

- The impulses are given in different parts of the passive person's body with distinct qualities being indicated through touch, i.e.,

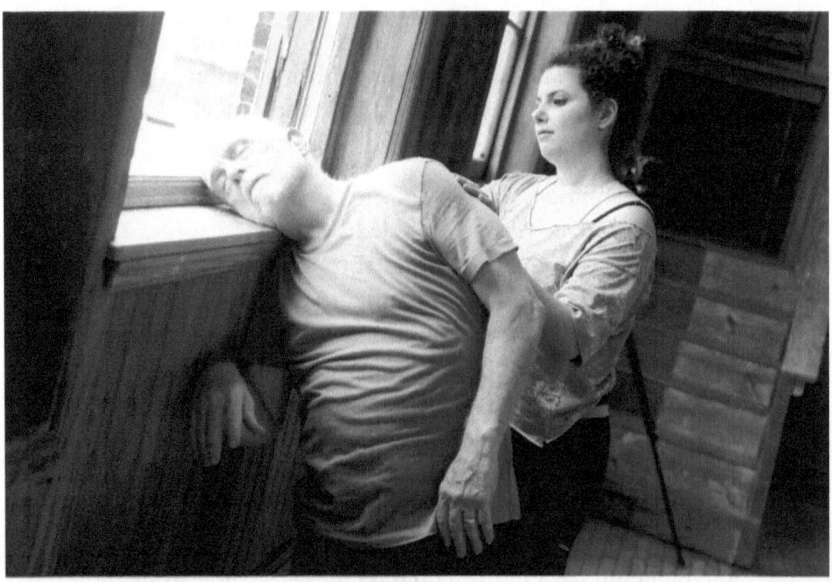

Gary Gray and Sophia Trovato interact in the Active Passive Dance, Friday Night Workshop, 2015 (photograph courtesy Bill Hebert).

direction or dynamic. The passive person moves with the impulses and lets the movements grow and travel through the body. Eventually the movement fades, and another impulse is given.

Reflection

Brigitta—*We know that human beings and all living creatures are in need of touch. We live in a culture that has reduced touch, for the most part, to either violence or sexuality. Yet, the spectrum of touch is diverse and versatile. In our culture, animals are more often kindly touched than our best friends or family. Movement and dance have a special place in the domain of touch. Dancers use their bodies as instruments of communication, using the ability to recognize sensation and cultivate awareness. Most often, it is transferred from one teacher to the next, playing out as an instructor's own awareness of contact and of partnering was cultivated, and enlightened at the time.*

Manfred—*As part of Young Audiences, a program that sends artists and companies into schools for performances and workshops, a group of Group Motion Company dancers was sent into a Youth Prison. We were led into basement room with concrete floors and bare walls and asked to wait there for the "kids." We were trying to picture who they would be and what we could do with them.*

On our way down, we had seen some "teachers" walking around with sticks.

When they walked in, eight or ten boys aged 10–14, clearly not very excited about this, the ideas of what to do with them and how to make them move were not coming up easily. Who had ever thought that this could work? So we tried some things, performed for them, showed them the mirror exercise and I don't remember what else. Nothing clicked or worked.

Finally, we demonstrated the Active-Passive Dance. Surprisingly they showed interest in that and soon wanted to try this themselves. And they did and really seemed to enjoy themselves, moving each other, making statues, having control over or giving up control to someone in this peaceful trust and touch exercise. All this happening in a Juvenile Delinquent Center.

In a totally different context many years earlier, Group Motion was performing its second major dance piece since our arrival in the U.S. called The Great Theater of Oklahoma Is Calling You, *based on Kafka's novel,*

Amerika. *It was at the Loeb auditorium of New York University, and at the end of the performance, the audience was invited to come onto the stage space and join in the Active-Passive Dance. Many of them did, prompting a dance critic to write, "Group Motion presented one of the most successful dance games with audience participation...."*

The Active Passive-Dance concluded also every assembly program Group Motion Company did at numerous schools ranging from kindergarten to high schools, from public to private schools of all sizes and formats. It has never failed to engage the audience and participants at a high level. Often upon leaving the school after our program, we saw kids practicing the Active-Passive in the schoolyard on their own.

Activation

For 2 to 20 participants.
With live music.
This structure can be seen as an evolution of the Active-Passive form.

One-on-One Activation

- Two people divide into an activator and a to-be-activated one, a giver and a receiver.
- The activator takes a moment to focus the passive person's presence, physically and emotionally.
- S/he then begins to sculpt and shape the other's body, following their perception of the physical and energetic receptivity of the passive person, as well as their own creativity.
- The activator will create different shapes and forms, and modify them until they feel complete with the form, shape, or character that they have created. The activator can also give a verbal idea along with the shape or character that will feed the movement realization.
- Then, the activator gives a signal, perhaps a clap, or a verbal cue, upon which the receiver begins to activate, bringing the still form into movement, into life.

It is important that the receiver takes a moment to listen and to feel the particular form, shape and its energy and expression in his or her body, before s/he begins to move.

The movement realization, or the dancing of this form that s/he has been given will maintain the essential and primary characteristics of it,

Activation Dance with Nina Sherak (*standing*) and Kristin Narcowich, Friday Night Workshop, 2015 (photograph courtesy Bill Hebert).

while moving it, exploring its life/dance potential, extending it, creating alterations. Without having to keep the exact form, the dance wants to stay true to the essence of the original.

- A signal of the observing activator will create the next form to activated and so on.
- After a few turns, the two people will exchange roles.

Variation

- This game/structure can be practiced in a group setting, with several pairs happening at the same time.

- Once they have been created, the facilitator may lead all of the still forms into a simultaneous dance, through a specific signal, where the now activated forms meet and interact and play with each other.
- Another signal ends the dance in a freeze.

Participants' Reflection

"At Group Motion, I learned giving weight and trust while maintaining my own balance."

"During the dance I kept my eyes closed the whole time. I was walking on the floor and touching something hot and cold and skin and just feeling the vibration of the other person. It all became very strong inside. It felt like I was blind and sensing this for the first time."

"It transformed my day from frustration to peace, from depression and upset to love, and from isolation to a sense of connection and oneness."

Mirror

For 2 to any number of participants.
With or without music.

Darcy Lyons (*left*) and Nina Sherak practice the Mirror Dance, Friday Night Workshop, 2015 (photograph courtesy Bill Hebert).

- Two people face each other, either standing or sitting. Establish eye contact using peripheral vision.
- To begin, move slowly, only changing facial expressions, using each other as a mirror. In doing so, alternate leading and following.
- Gradually, add the whole body, without touching.
- As two people develop their dance, they can change distance, being very close or very far away from one another. They can move in any way that allows synchronicity with each other. As the dance unfolds and the movers observe each other closely, guiding or following one another, there is a sense of tuning in, of breathing simultaneously, and of energy exchange.

Reflection

Brigitta—*The Mirror game is a structure that is widely used in the tradition of theater improvisation, in Dance Movement Therapy, and in other therapeutic settings. There is a wide variety in the ways it is played and taught. Its simple ritualistic form is easily understood, and the dance is created anew each time.*

Certain movement habits or trends may become apparent during this

Mirror Dance with Sophia Trovato (*left*) and Andrea Clearfield, Friday Night Workshop, 2015 (photograph courtesy Bill Hebert).

dance. For example, preferences for following, leading, or noticing conflict may arise. Participants may also sense their own anticipation, surrender, frustration, and judgment during this encounter. We can notice which role we feel more comfortable in with the other person. We can recognize which area of our body feels more or less at ease to be moved. Altogether, these elements offer valuable insights into patterns of relationships. They may be emotional and relevant to age and gender. The mirror dance teaches a non-competitive and playful interaction. It also promotes a sense of oneness with another person, without sexual overtones.

Closing Your Eyes

For 2 to any number of participants.
With or without music.

- Face a partner; make eye contact.
- Direct your seeing from various places of the body, for example: bottom of your feet, back of your head, space of your heart.
- Instructions will ask you to close your eyes after a short time of such seeing.
- The instructor may say: " Perceive the other with your eyes closed."
- Begin to move from this perception of the other.
- Come to a place of stillness as you open your eyes. Gently part and make eye contact with somebody else.
- It may be repeated a number of times.

Reflection

Brigitta—*This form of attention, seeing from an inward sense, allows for the "window of your eyes" to open without judgment, letting in what wants to come in. The observer will see a shift of energy, people moving in subtle, inwardly directed ways. Often you will see people bow as they part from each other. This sequence of instruction may be repeated twice or three times, and most often has led to the structure, "Moving or Being Still."*

Self Portrait Dance

A solo movement structure.
With live music.

- Each person designs seven sculptural movement expressions of different aspects of themselves.
- The seven forms are assigned to different spots on the stage space, reflective of where they would be most effectively expressed and perceived. They may, or may not be named with what they represent or mean. In a variation, a verbal expression may be attached to two or three of the seven poses.
- In step one of the process, they are shown one by one in a "lights off, lights on" technique. (When the instructor calls "Lights off," everyone observing closes their eyes, while the dancer changes the pose. When "Lights on" is called, everyone opens their eyes.)
- In step two, the dancer will "connect the dots," meaning that s/he will move through the map of still sculptures to create a continuous dance, in which each form informs the movement character and quality, as it travels and transforms on the way to the next still form. The completed dance will then be performed with live music.

Variation

- A group of solos may also be performed at the same time. When shown collectively the co-existing sculptures or dances often provide unexpected relationships, compositions, and dynamics. The live music will hold the shared space.

Reflection

Manfred—*These haiku like portrait creations offer both a playful and contemplative reflection on the body language and movement signatures, drawing the inner and outer contours of a person into the space. When turned into a dance, it can provide surprising insights, discoveries, and movement inventions.*

Solo Dance/Writing

For 2 players.
With live music.
Two players choose between being a dancer or a writer/observer. They will be reversing their roles in the second round of play.

- Phase One: For one minute, timed by the facilitator, the dancer engages in spontaneous, authentic movement, following one's own impulses without pre-meditation, while the writer observers and takes notes. These notes can be descriptive, associative, or metaphoric in nature, and can use nouns, verbs, adverbs, or adjectives in an immediate act of tracking the mover.
- Phase Two: For one and a half minutes, the two players go into separate spaces.
- The dancer engages in recapturing the movement progression, remembering and re-tracking it as authentically as possible, but without worrying about total accuracy.
- The writer engages in fleshing out his/her notes, embellishing and organizing them into coherent, but not necessarily linear, or logical form. The writer uses his/her visual, mental, and emotional recall, as well as reflective or interpretive elements of testimony, but without watching the dancer.
- Phase Three: The dancer and the writer share and perform the movement and the writing simultaneously, in full awareness of listening and watching, perceiving each other. Both the delivery of the movement and of the text can take creative liberty in terms of dynamics, timing, and even sequencing—still staying true to the original. The dancer can pause, sustain, repeat, or even alter movements. The writer may do the same, animate the reading, even sing the words, in spontaneous and creative interaction with each other's performance.
- In Phase Three, performance of the movement and spoken word could be accompanied by live, improvised music.

Reflection

Manfred—In the Solo Dance/ Writing Game, the co-creative potency of this process is fueled by the duality of dependence and independence that is at work, the coincidental and yet non-coincidental relationship between the nonverbal and the verbal expressions that are woven together, drawing from both the conscious and the subconscious sources of the performers. With live improvised music, these poem/dances provide a delightful insight into each person's perceptions and their associative resonances, and give the outside observers their own space of reflection.

Dialogue

For 2 to 30 people.
With live music.

- Two people are standing or sitting facing each other.
- One of the two will begin to move in relation to the stillness, reacting to the other. At the point of having completed his/her "statement," s/he will become still, holding the last shape or gesture.
- At this point, the other person will begin to move/speak in response and in relation to the shape or gesture, the listening, the negative space, the form, energy, or expression of the first person, until his/her statement comes to completion and stillness.
- And so on.
- The "speaking" person may also use sound with their movement. Or the "listener" may choose sound as an expression of witnessing, or both; the moving and the still person can be sounding at the same time.
- There can be a number of dialogues taking place at the same time.
- Live music will be the holder of the shared space.

Variation

- The Dialogue Game can be played by groups of three or four. The same principles of "speaking" and "listening" and moving and being still apply. Like with the dialogue in pairs, there can be several conversations in groups of three or four going on at the same time, in the same place. Here too, live music can be the holder of the larger, shared space.

Reflection

Manfred—*The creation of the Dialogue Game dates back to some time in the Seventies. I remember it emerging in a rehearsal, first in the form of a "Broken Mirror," and later in a form of a movement conversation—"speaking and listening," "call and answer," taking turns in moving and being still.*

In many ways, this structure is one of the purest manifestations of movement as a language of expression and communication. In this wondrous change between stillness and movement, talking and listening, whole stories or scenarios of relationships between players can be created in this intimate back and forth of communication.

Numerous comments have been made by participants about the fact that this dance allows for the powerful possibility of "talking to strangers" intimately, of getting to know the other in ways that would be impossible to do with just words.

The trust and playfulness that is at the core of this agreement of talking and listening to each other through the language of movement are magic wands that open the doors to a way of dreaming. We are journeying together into the unknown or familiar, imagined or remembered, private or dramatic, ancient or futuristic territories of shared, spontaneous, creation.

Connected to Strings

For 1 or more players.
With or without music.
Visualize the body as connected to strings at all different points, between head and heel. Imagine these strings to be pulled or released whenever and wherever you choose. The pulling and releasing may happen with various degrees of force, or different qualities, and may affect one or two, or several parts of the body simultaneously. It may take you off-center, down to the ground or back up. It may happen in small and minute ways, slow or fast, or in big and whole body motions. At all times, the dancer is compelled to move by the imaginary strings, as if s/he is operated by an outside source, even though that source is located within yourself. It is an active-passive dance between your mind, your breath, and your body. The puppet and puppeteer, the marionette and its master are within the same being.

Variations
- One may apply the imagining of everyday actions or situations, or the inducement of different emotional states to the act of being moved by the strings.
- There can also be interactivity with other puppet beings, in the form of mirroring, dialoguing, or even physical contact, to the point of synchronization or entanglement of imaginary strings.

Reflection

Manfred—*Even though Being Attached to Strings seems to be an exercise in isolation of body parts, it is really a whole body experience, a body/mind/spirit integration. It is also a heightened state of listening, of surrender to the impulses from within and their external manifestations. Henrich von Kleist, the German poet of the romantic era, wrote a famous essay "Uber das Marionettentheater" in which he defines the movement of the marionettes as a state of grace, as one of being moved by "god," or the spirit, or the energy. It is safe to say, that he did not envision the marionette to actually manifest dance in the human body. But in a strange and beautiful way, in his play, the characters and their actions are being moved by mysterious strings, connected to their subconscious, or to an inner knowing that pulls them into a state of grace, and dancing even in tragic circumstances.*

Self-Activation

For any number of players.
With live music.

- Out of a process of guided simultaneous dancing by all participants, with changing focus on various parts of the body as points of initiation, the facilitator will call a 'Freeze."
- Each participant will freeze in a shape and form of their own momentary physical and emotional status. This "shape and form" will become the "activating" agent of the dance, as the dancers are asked to bring it into movement.
- As these dances have evolved and found their own life and character, the facilitator will ask that they are danced with a change of a particular quality, emotional charge, or dynamic. "Dance this dance sharp and angular ... with lightness ... with a feeling of anger ... with a sense of remembering ... with sadness... with contentment ... etc."
- While adding each dynamic, the dancers are to maintain the original shape and form in the respective variations. These solo dances can be led into interaction with each other, and thus become a duet of the two different original "forms" danced in the same quality, or with the same emotional charge.
- After a series of changes of duet partners, the dancers will be guided to stay with one other partner and begin to mirror each other's movement.

Reflection

Manfred—This structure is frequently inserted into the Friday Night Workshop. There, as in other contexts of practice, it provides a rich experience of movement discovery, as the unexpected frozen forms are put into life. There is a freeing from pre-programmed technical or routine movement vocabulary at work. When these dances are put into interaction with one another, an expanded level of authentic movement communication can be reached. For example: two movement characters dancing in a sharp and angular fashion, or with a sense of sadness, or with surprise.

Self-Activation Character Movement

These exercises serve the purpose of extended movement in the creation of an individual character.

- The player will choose between the following parameters as a sub-textual focus to be infused into the character's movement and voice: (a) a color; (b) a texture (smooth, liquid, solid, fuzzy); (c) an element; (d) an animal (e) an imaginary past life form...
- S/he makes the choice of one or several of these foci in accordance with their interpretation of the character, and lets their physicalization be informed by them.

As an example, Franz Kafka's "Report to an Academy" tells the story of how the speaker, a former ape, transformed himself into a human being. With the choices of parameters being obvious in this case, the actor faces the challenge of a delicate balance between manifesting the ape's past and the human's present embodiment.

Variation

- The player delivering a memorized monologue is asked to move in a random and rapid pace, letting the body's impulses manifest in an uncensored, unrelated way, without trying to make sense or be meaningful, letting the speaking and the movement exist independently from one another.

Reflection

Manfred—This exercise reveals that as random or unrelated to intent or purpose the movement might appear to be, choices are definitely made, even if on a subconscious level. It reminds of the way children tell their stories animated by their uncensored body movements.

Breathing Movement

For any number of dancers.
With or without music.
The purpose of this exercise is to become conscious of the breath. A sequence of inhalations and exhalations with a definite rhythm is assigned. Use a frame drum to give the timing.

- On a count of 4: inhale on 4, exhale chopped syncopation; inhale on 4; exhale on 4.
- Then instructor changes the counts: inhale on 2, exhale on 2; inhale on 2, exhale on 2. Or, inhale on 4; exhale on a short "pahh" sound. Start over.
- Try using sounds, vocalizing and amplifying your breath. Stop and breathe in stillness for four counts.

It really can be played with different timing, and it could also be reversed. There is room for play in how the instructor develops the sequences of chopping or even breath, depending on perceived needs of the group.

Let the movement of your body follow the natural expansion and contraction of your breath. As your movement becomes more and more defined, you will experience *being* rather than *doing* your breath.

- Dancers can then listen and breathe in stillness for 8 counts.
- Invite the dancers to breathe in sync with their movement.
- Invite the dancers to find their own rhythm within the frame of the given beat.

Variation One

- Find a partner and vocalize/move alternating turns, coming into a dialogue of movement/sound and stillness/listening.
- Do the same with focus on rhythm.

In everything you do, accompany it with subtle sounds and listen for their emotional content, their message, their quality, their texture, and meaning.

Variation Two

- Standing close together in a group.
- Learn the breath rhythm as your instructor recites it out loud.

As each dancer understands the rhythm s/he begins to move with eyes closed, still repeating the breath rhythm.

Reflection

Brigitta—*When a child is first born and takes a breath, it is separating itself from the body of the mother and connecting fully to its own. A new life and consciousness has begun. With this first breath, a movement passes through the body of the child, an incredible sensation of life—the first dance of breath, sound, and movement together. When we dance, we are aiming for this togetherness.*

As I begin to dance, I experience another world, another life. My body is moved, bent, stretched, held, shaken, exploded, vibrated. I am lifted up, crashed down, whirled around. Who is doing it? I am not doing it. I am given it and my breath is giving it to me. It is moving me. My breath, through it, I experience my life.

Final Reflections on Solo/Duet Forms

Brigitta—Solo and duet forms are enacted in a multitude of dance styles, such as folk or ethnic dances, ballroom, classical or modern dance and postmodern or street dance. Group Motion has found its own style of communicating in Solo and Duet forms, as demonstrated in these games.

The Solo exercises explore inner landscapes of the self, stimulated by particular simple prompts. As with Connected to Strings, I imagine the strings pulling me. There is no personification behind it, yet an invisible force is taking the lead pulling, letting go of, drawing or tugging parts of my body, pulling me into the space and may even connecting me to other dancers' "strings" in a tangle, or twisting towards or away from another. I let my imagination create the partnership. It is a training in focus. I focus on kinesthetic sensations. It is a form of self-programing, like self-hypnosis.

In the Self Portrait, I explore landscapes of myself through various ages, connecting with events, memories, and images of the self, weaving them into a random tapestry of life events. Containing intense moods or feelings, I embody their textures, colors through sequences of movement, through repetition, their relation into space, tempo or stillness. The initial gestures will find their form, including a resonance, rhythm or melody or silence. In this way, I string together a sequence of bits into a multi-animated dance, a spontaneous presentation, a composition of pieces of my past, my present and projections into the future. This can be cartoonishly funny, or deeply revealing.

The Solo/Writing Game also proceeds in various stages. This structure offers a delightful space for dialogue between two people, a witness/writer and a spontaneously moving dancer. The object being observed is also influenced by this observation. It is fascinating how it creates a heightened sense of awareness of intensified self-observation, which is reinforced by the one-minute repetition of this dance. The writer's role offers a practice of empathy. Tuning to the dance kinesthetically and without judgment, s/he will align with the dancer by using words and symbolic language to illustrate what s/he feels and sees, adding an additional layer to the story. Two people being intimately yet playfully connected for this moment in time, it may feel like sharing a fleeting dream.

With Breathing Movement, I tune into my breath, making it audible. I become focused and get in touch with deep levels of myself, emotionally, physically and spiritually. As I make my breath audible, I begin to create and listen to the rhythm and nuances of it. It is a lead-in for sound making, for vocalizing. Amplifying the breath, engaging vocal cords, I begin to hear my voice and aim at various frequencies, high and low. In doing so, I can feel the resonance in different areas of my own body. It includes the movements of my face. This is not about singing, but rather resembling a spectrum of our ancestral animal nature, evoking the sound quality of a primeval language that is invigorating, empowering and transformative. Amplifying the breath and leading into vocalization in a vast scale of emotions, I explore a range from whispering to shouting. This exercise of listening and of empowering voice can be a practice that I engage on my own, or as a dialogue, or with a group. In this practice, I sensitize myself towards listening, and I learn about differentiating the scale—from audible breath and minimalist movement—to full out primal utterance and powerful articulation. The self-expression can be dramatic or melodious, musical or theatrical, bewildering and comical.

The Duet forms take our focus outside the self to engage with another. In the context of dance, we are "allowed" to be in close contact to another body and to be in touch. We know that a one on one relationship is our primary experience of self, of how we get to know ourselves. To be reflected, to be heard, to be validated, understood and touched is essential for the development of the human being. A child who is held with loving hands and comforted with loving touch will learn do the same, as we learn by example. Touch carries messages about pleasure, sexuality, dislike, anger, love and fear. The growing embryo is held in its tight container, reassured by the mother's heartbeat, her voice, the rhythm of her steps as she walks. Any of her movements become part of the developing sensory perception of the infant, while the emotional connection and the energy of thought are related through her breath, the firing of nerve impulses, digestive movements and the subtle rhythms of the organs. During my pregnancies, I experienced the closeness of the infant inside the womb, the subtle movements as a form of being touched from the inside.

At this time and in the culture we live in, it is not an unusual phenomenon to feel starved for love, touch and tenderness. Yet, we are in need of touch, and our hands are instruments of communication. The cultural parameter has reduced touch for the most part to a handshake, a pat on the back, or to the other extremes of violence and sexuality. Commercialization of sexuality, and the constant reminder that touch can be dangerous, screams at children and young people through images and the daily news. Renditions of sexuality through porn and media have trivialized touch. Yet, we also know of the comforting touch of handholding and the calming touch of the palm sliding. We know of healing touch that is energizing, supporting, stretching, lifting, cleansing. We know of touch that is violent, pushing, slapping, spanking, punching, teasing and killing. Touch is not something that stays on the surface; on the contrary, it goes deep.

Since dancers use their bodies as instruments of communication, the ability to recognize sensation and cultivate awareness through touch is essential. Yet, even in dance education it is not necessarily a conscious subject, but more often subtly transferred from one teacher to the next. It plays out in the ways a dancer's skills and awareness are trained and passed along. In the context of dance, there are many shades of touch; the spectrum of touch is on a wide scale, versatile and beautiful. I am aware of my own longing for touch. The pleasure of leaning on somebody, sitting close to someone, holding hands, walking together, it synchronizes our breath and empathic understanding of the other person and can give us the feeling of comfort of belonging, of harmony, safety and of caring. Dancing, I can get in touch with the men or women and gender becomes insignificant. It is a different kind of touch. It is functional, balancing, supporting weight, holding on for various kinds of lifts and figurations. Like its 1970s dance cousin, Contact Improvisation, our forms utilize gravity, momentum, and inertia, but the Group Motion intention is to always go beyond the unit of two, to ultimately join individuals and pairs into ever increasing units.

Each of the Group Motion duet forms emphasizes a different focus. All of the duet structures and games play with leading or following in one form or another. It turns out that even in the following/leading paradigm we never just lead or follow. There is a sense of fluidity, a back and forth, and degree of influence being influenced by the other. Not unlike in conversation when we speak with someone, we hear ourselves in relation to the one who listens. This too plays itself out in the dialogue of dance.

The Active-Passive Dance of Group Motion evolved in the context of working with professional dancers and untrained movers in the attempt to safely explore, interact and play. What is easy for a dancer is not self-evident to the untrained individual. It may appear extraordinary, breathtaking and even scary for ordinary "normal" men or women who have never met before to have permission to play and trust another, touching and being touched. The Active-Passive Game is about exploring shades of touch in a safe and caring environment. From a light touch of hands to a firm touch of holding a hand or a head or a shoulder, a sense of sculpting, to guiding, or being guided, from being danced to the flow of music to being held or patted on the back. Oftentimes, you may find yourself being swung around or pulled across the floor. The variations are endless and always guided from a sense of comfort and respect for personal boundaries, engaged from a perspective of love and caring as this dance evolves. In that sense, it is a delightful form of a dance between two strangers, and maybe an eye-opener for partners and friends.

I think of it as a contribution to peace in the world, because when you engage in the Active-Passive dance with a stranger and receive all this loving and caring energy you can only be peaceful. I have heard people say many times how it transformed their day.

The Mirror Game is exploring how we see ourselves in the eyes of the other. How do we respond to and or lead the person in front of us? The rational mind sinks away making room for the intuitive. Action and reaction become obvious, visible, and take on form. We know from research how the infant learns about language. As the mother speaks to her infant child, her sounds and intentions, and the emotions behind those sounds are absorbed, not only through the sound perception, but also through the body. The infant can be seen mirroring those sounds with ever so small and an intrinsic sense of movement. Her/his learning is holistic, body/mind/emotion are in concert, in coordination, in harmony or dissonance accordingly. There is no judgment, but rather just what IS SO. It is always about the experience of giving and receiving. Without question, we take what comes and transform it, "We go from there." We see it reflected in nature, as it is our nature.

In Closing Your Eyes, I go deeper yet. Standing or sitting with your partner in eye contact, and then closing your eyes, as instructed, I receive an impression of my partner without judgment or question. I remember sensing, seeing, the child, seeing her/him at the age of 3 or 5 or 8, an image of that child. S/he is moving, gesturing, relating in a certain way. Closing your eyes and seeing the other from a space of the heart, opens the self to that heart-space, that fourth chakra energy. What kind of dance will evolve from such a space? There is no concept of a right or wrong. But rather whatever movement moves me. I have heard participants share about this experience, that when they were looking into someone's eyes and closing their eyes, they felt drawn into the other person. It was a profound and touching experience, something we do not usually allow ourselves to do, make deeply felt contact with a stranger, without wanting anything.

Circle

Dance is an experience
Dance is a form of life
Dance is speaking from your soul-through your body
Where dance is, there is happiness
Dance is effortless
When you dance, you are not dancing, but it is
Dancing you
Dance is healing
Dance is the singing of the breath
Dance is the state of being high
Dance is important
Dance is an expression of how to be
Dance is interplanetary
Dance is without fear
The grass is dancing
The trees are dancing
The water is dancing
The stars are dancing
Having seen dance is like waking from a dream
Dance is reality when you are in it
Dance is taking you where you want to be
Dance is a form of love
When you dance you are without name, you are energy
Passing through, flowing, merging, connecting, transforming
Dance is
Dance

—Brigitta

Impulse

For 6 to 20 or more participants.
Without music.

- The group stands in a circle, arms distance apart, and facing center. It is important that everyone in the group can see the whole circle.
- One person begins with a movement/gesture impulse, with or without sound.
- The impulse, like a chain reaction, is repeated around the circle, one dancer at a time, in one direction.
- As the impulse travels around the circle, repeat the gesture/movement/sound as quickly and as exactly as possible. Let it travel once around the circle, ending with the one who started it.
- Continue immediately with the next person, beginning a new impulse.

Variation

- Allow for the impulse to change slightly as it travels several times, for example three times around the circle. Or let it travel until the energy of the impulse fades to stillness. From there, anyone can begin a new one.
- In another variation, the impulse is repeated by the entire group, in unison, two or three times. Each participant takes a turn to initiate, going around the circle.

Participants engage in the Impulse Dance, Group Motion Retreat, Great Sand Dunes National Park, Colorado, 2008 (photograph courtesy Colin Harvey).

Depending on the kind of impulse, it may evolve into a wave as it speeds around the circle.

Reflection

Manfred—It was before the famous stadium wave came into fashion during bigger sports events that we practiced the Impulse Circle as one of Group Motions' core structures. Its unique feature of chain reaction, or domino effect, was applicable to groups of all sizes, from crowds to intimate circles of four to five people. One of those intimate circles provided a life changing experience for me, and my immediate family.

Brigitta and I returned to Germany from America for the first time; this must have been 1973. We visited my parents and my older sister at their home in Pinneberg, a small town outside of Hamburg. It was around Christmas when we arrived, and on New Year's Eve, we sat around the table after dinner, when someone, I believe it was Brigitta, suggested we do a movement game.

My parents were in their eighties. My father was not walking too well at the time, so we decided to do the Impulse Circle sitting in the circle around the table. It lasted only a short time, a few rounds of movement impulse waves around this five family member circle. However, some of the impulses that my mother and my father rendered are engraved forever in my memory. I saw their psyches, their child natures. We all saw each other in a way that we had never seen each other before.

The next morning, my father, who had not really understood or approved of my choice of dance as a profession, came to me and said that now he understood something about that. He had experienced with his 85-year-old body and spirit the power of movement, and the healing language of dance, probably for the first time.

Name Game

For 6–12 participants.
Without music.
The Name Game is very much like the Impulse Game.

- The group stands in a circle formation, facing center.
- The objective is to use your name along with a gesture or movement.

- One person starts using his/her name as a source. The sound of the name maybe shifted and modified, and is expressed together with a movement.
- Next, it is passed along from person to person in the circle. Moving in one direction, it travels around once, ending with the person who started.
- In turn, the next person in the circle will use his/her name with a particular gesture or movement, passing it along. It continues, until each person in the circle has had a turn. In this way, all participants in the circle will get to know everyone else, attaining a sense of each person by embodying their name and expression.

Variation

- Instead of letting each name travel around from one to the next, the name is repeated two or three times simultaneously by everyone in the group. Each participant has a turn to initiate, using he/her name, as it is going around the circle.

Reflection

Brigitta—*This structure is well known in the Dance/Movement Therapy context, as a way to introduce oneself and to "break the ice." Its nonverbal expressiveness can be hilariously funny and insightful. Its unpremeditated, spontaneous actions reflect on the participants' states of mind, their dispositions, and their psyches. In a therapeutic context, it can offer ways to relieve tension and offer leads towards the transformation of behavior while building self-confidence.*

Looking back at a video recording of such a name game circle from 20 years back, I'm amazed at the clarity of each person's "movement signature."

It is a delightful way to play with children and with various populations of all ages, even while sitting in chairs. In my work with the elderly in an Adult Day Care, we would play the Name Game.

Adding

For 5 to 12 participants.
With or without music.

Circle—Adding

Participants stand in a circle at arms' length from each other, facing each other.

- One person initiates a movement or brief phrase of movements, with or without sound, or a word, repeating it, while pausing between each repetition.
- After observing, the second person joins into the same movement/sound with the first person. Both repeat the first movement three times in unison, and then the second person adds their own movement/sound, both of which are repeated in sequence.
- The next person, and then eventually everyone in the circle, one by one, joins in, repeating the sequence and adding on a new movement. The added movement can be a continuation of the one before, or in contrast to it.
- Eventually, everyone in the group enters, one by one, adding a movement/sound to the sequence. It can go around the circle once, twice, or three times, depending on the size of the group and their abilities. As a result, the movement phrase will get longer with each added part, and can become rather complex.

Variation: Adding Game Themes

The Adding Game can be abstract, dance oriented, or theatrical. It can also be played including words.

- The Adding Game can be played with a theme chosen as an inspiration. Suggested themes are elements—water, earth, fire, air, ice, or seasons—spring, winter, fall, summer. Other possibilities for themes are emotions, or states of mind, or more abstract ones like colors or textures.
- There is a unique quality that occurs in the circle, coherent phrases are created from everyone's input so it becomes instant poetry with instant choreography. At the end of playing the game, you will arrive at a composition of steps/movements/ expressions that are linked together like a phrase. It is surprising, time after time, to see how cohesion and innovative forms evolve.

Variation: Adding Game Open Forum

- In a variation of the Adding Game, after several repetitions of the entire sequence in a circle formation, the circle may be dis-

solved and dancers invited to move into the space, taking on various directions.
- While keeping their movement phrase intact, the dancers are prompted to form new constellations with each other. In this new development, numerous formations can evolve. The accuracy and unison of the repeated phrase, its dynamic and nuances of expression are maintained, unless instructions encourage change.

Advanced versions of this structure can be played. Once the phrase is completed it may be used for improvisational exploration or development of choreography. Participants improvise using phrase sequences, like a theme and variation, taking fragments of the phrase out of order or in repetition. In addition, various Adding Games can be played with sequences interfacing each other. One example of this is a mandala, where different sequences are played in concentric circles.

Or, instead of forming a circle, participants can start at the periphery of the room. One person then begins the first movement in the center of the room. Then a second person will join the first and add on, until everyone has added to the sequence. This version offers more opportunities for spatial innovations, making use of movements traveling across the floor.

The Adding Game can also be done sitting on the floor, on chairs, or around a table.

Reflection

Brigitta—*The Adding Game is an original Group Motion structure and has a broad range of options for how it can be played. It could be abstract, dance-oriented, or highly theatrical, or it can even be played verbally. There is a unique quality that occurs in the circle; coherent phrases are created from everyone's input, so it becomes instant poetry, instant choreography.*

"Dreaming" or thinking up dance structures has become my playful obsession. Riding the bus on my way back home from teaching dance at the Valery Bettis Dance Studio in NYC, I visualized dances, formations of dancers, their spatial orientations, choreographic patterns, their architecture and dynamics. The Adding Game was one of those structures that emerged in this context.

The Adding Game is an exemplary structure for instant choreography.

At the end of playing the game, you will arrive at a composition of steps/movements/expressions that are linked together. It is still surprising, time after time, to see how cohesive and innovative forms evolve.

Final Reflections on Circle Forms

Brigitta—The circle is an ancient sacred form of coming together in celebration. In nature, circular forms dominate, from the circling of planets to the images of moon and earth, from the shape of flowers, leaves and nests to seashells, nuts, stones and fruits. We as human beings are circular, our organs and our cells. And, we know in the context of dance, from ancient times through the Middle Ages, from the Renaissance to modern times, circle dances have persevered in numerous forms. The circle implies trust in connection. We can see each other in a circle, walk towards and away from each other. We may hold hands and or circle around each other. Circle dances are associated with rituals and shamanic traditions. In the context of Group Motion, circle dances are also about giving and receiving, about communication and community.

In the process of the Impulse Game, spontaneously giving or receiving a movement impulse, a gesture, or a sound-movement to the person next to you, is like a gift or an offering. Standing in the circle, knowing that each person will have a turn to initiate such an offering, I notice the suspense. The mind wants to jump ahead and be prepared when it is your turn. I am being watched, I am being seen by everyone in the circle. I reveal something about myself making this gesture or sound. As I was looking at that video recording of the Impulse Dance from 20 years ago, I recognized the dancers, friends, their familiar faces and their gestures from that moment in time. I saw who we were at this moment. There is a feeling, an emotion behind that dance that was absorbed by everyone and confirmed by the repetition. We visibly surprised ourselves, and each other. It is a different kind of small ritual, differentiating Group Motion from other circle dances where steps and gestures are predetermined and learned through repetition, even from one generation to the next.

I was excited to witness a ritual of a circle dance at the Hopi Reservation some time in the Eighties. There were older folks and children participating in the circle, and the little ones picked up the steps and gestures as they went along. We learned that everyone over the generations knew their meanings, and they continued those steps and gestures, honoring their ritualistic significance.

Another Group Motion circle classic, The Name Game is widely known. Using your name in connection with a gesture, this dance-game contributes to sharpen our first impression of another person. We will remember the one who made a big step, who jumped, or made a funny face, together with speaking her or his name. The combination of physical and emotional energy leaves an impression while being playful and fun. It will aid in taking away the anxiety or uneasiness participants may experience, and can open the space for further interaction down the road. By showing your own vulnerability and seeing others doing the same, participants experience a sense of ease and trust towards those they just met. Maybe they saw their nervousness, or their foolishness, or shyness, and now understand that they are not alone.

The Adding Game is one of my favored structures and it turned out to have multiple applications and variations. It is a game of learning dance/movement vocabulary and of practicing awareness of form and composition/choreography. Right from the start, it was introduced as a structure that integrated movement with voice. Vocalizing your movement you notice how breath and expression are linked. Listening and embodying go together.

For example, we choose a theme like WATER.

In a circle of eight, spontaneously each dancer will find her/his own expression of water, one at a time, in order of a clockwise direction in the circle. For one it may be a wave, for another it may be a dripping or splashing movement. The dancers sense of rhythm and timing plays into the process. Each dancer is making a contribution to the whole of the final movement phrase. It evolves and becomes more and more refined and clear in the process of repetition. In this process of training your movement memory towards composition, we rely on each individual in the circle, and learn commitment towards the accuracy of performance. As each dancer offers a piece of the puzzle, s/he is also responsible for maintaining the authenticity of it for everyone else to mirror and adopt it correctly. It makes it easy to remember each gesture. You do not have to worry about remembering. You will be able to see and hear each movement repeatedly as it is going around in the circle.

In variation, we can play the game with 2 or 3 or more circles at the same time. They can be separate in the space or eventually stacked into each other, like the rings in a pond when you throw a stone. It is like a living mandala. Each circle has its own rhythm, its distinct dynamic and movement patterns. Their timing and spatial elements differ; yet all are fitting magically together. It reminds me of how in nature, each plant finds its color, height and shape, and they compliment one another beautifully, as they grow near each other.

In an extension of the Adding Game and towards the process of choreography with advanced students we may dissolve the circles. The dancers continue their sequences and stay in visual proximity of one another. They can change their spatial formation while maintaining their movement phrases, accompanied by live or prerecorded music. The Adding Game allows for countless variations, depending on the size of a group and the number of groups in space, and their respective themes.

I have used this structure with children ages eight to eighteen to create dances of various lengths, and with a wide range of ideas coming from the children. Rather than demonstrating steps for them to follow, they follow each other and learn how to invent and remember movement during the process. Skills and ideas are shared on levels according to age and experience. There is no competition. Each child can offer her/his special move and find her own natural expression. The Adding Game is one of collective creation and of shared adventure.

Relevant to the four levels of influences and embodiment: physical, emotional, spiritual and social, we can see the following implications of the circle form. Physically—it is about orientation in space, the space between each other, the skill of holding a circle. Moving into random space, we develop a sense of all around orientation in space and how and when to change our direction. It is also about learning to be a part of a group, and we learn movement vocabulary by way of picking up each other's steps and gestures. We learn about rhythm and timing and their connection to breath and effort, and about finding balance between slow and fast, action and stillness. Spiritually-we learn about being focused and present, listening inwardly and outwardly. It is a training for expanding awareness, and trusting intuition. Emotionally—we get engaged with themes of personal, environmental, global issues and tune into each other's expressions. We learn to value emotionally charged expressions and trust our impulses and those of others. Socially—there is no need for competition as everyone finds his/her place within the whole. In this regard, it has implications for understanding the value of diversity and support and can lead to social change.

Space

I was sitting
My back against a tree
I heard from far away
A thousand voices laughing in the sky
As they came closer
I opened my eyes
Flocks of geese were dancing in flight
The Dance of the Returning Soul
The earth
My body
Opened wide

—Manfred

Areas

For 8 to 30 people.
With or without music.

- Divide the room into three or four areas with tape.
- Each area is assigned a theme or environment. For example: fire, water, earth, city, street, mirror, color, desert, emotion, pencils.
- Everybody begins to move in the same basic motion of walking, or jogging around the room. Participants stop at prearranged musical or vocal cues.
- Everyone will find him or herself in one of the areas, and begin moving again, transforming their movement according to the theme of the area. There are different ways to respond to a theme. For example, you can be in water, and you can also become water.
- People can move from one area to another at any time. When crossing the line, movements adapt to the theme accordingly.
- Participants can interact in the areas with each other.

Variation

- The whole group can start in one of the areas and travel together into a new area.

Reflection

Brigitta—*Areas was adopted from Improvisation Studies at the Mary Wigman School of Dance in Berlin. It was often introduced as a way to choose and explore themes. I remember themes of nature: water, air, earth, fire, falling leaves, wind/storm/rain. It is a wonderful structure to play with children of all ages.*

Crystallization

For 5 to 200 participants.
With or without music.

- People begin by walking or jogging randomly, with awareness of each other and the space around them.
- Upon impulse, one person freezes in a spontaneously created shape.
- Noticing the still person, everyone gradually moves to form the crystal by physically connecting in relation to the first person's particular shape.
- When everyone is connected, the crystal is formed.
- From this stillness, the originator of the frozen crystal begins a movement and sound impulse.
- As it is felt and heard, the impulse is repeated in unison, first by the dancer closest to the source and eventually to all, through the entire group. The impulse is repeated in unison.

The impulse spreads outward through the group like ripples from a stone thrown in water. As it continues to expand, the impulse breaks the physical connections of the group and people separate from each other, expanding outward as they continue the impulse.

When the expansion reaches its peak, the impulse will stop. From this moment of stillness, a new traveling motion begins. All dancers/movers will travel about in a particular way until the next person stops suddenly and initiates a new crystallization.

Crystallization Dance by retreat participants, Group Motion Retreat, Sarasota, Florida, 2007 (photograph courtesy Richard Marcus).

Variations

- More than one person may initiate a crystal at the same time, in which case the group members will randomly join the closest crystal.
- In another variation, participants do not resume the same basic motion after each crystal is formed. Instead, the person who started the crystal and gave the impulse also gives a new basic movement. This continues until the next crystal is formed.

Reflections

Brigitta and Manfred—*The Crystallization structure originated during a rehearsal with the company in the mid–Seventies. I remember observing the dancers during an improvisation and recognizing the pattern.*

Like the rings from a stone, you throw into a pond of water, the impulse spreads outward toward the periphery of the space. As each dancer now actively takes on the movement and sound of this impulse, you will also recognize a movement pattern. The pattern is expanding, the energy extending into the space, and reaches its highest point, ending again in stillness. From this perceived ending, the dancers start a new traveling motion. All dancers/movers will travel about in a unified way until the next person stops suddenly, and initiates a new crystallization. The traveling motion can vary each time. To start out, it may just be walking or jogging. A particular step—slow or fast, rhythmic or fluid is imitated by the particular leader of each respective crystal, and will be followed and sustained by the group. The traveling asks for spatial awareness. You can travel on your own, or join another or several others. The traveling pattern is engaging and fun, a dance of meeting and following. A repetitive step and quality of movement is sustained throughout the traveling phase.

If more than one dancer initiates a crystal at the same time, the group can proceed into two crystallizations, joining who ever s/he is closest to. This pattern can continue endlessly, with new formations and unpredictable shapes and impulses. Each time renewing itself, gaining momentum, shifting energy, creating, altering, contrasting space and time.

The structure of crystallization could stand as a symbol for Group Motion because it most visibly shows the interaction of our particleness and wholeness. Because one person gives the impulse to the whole group, there is a very strong experience of individuality. You learn to experience your individual strength while submitting to the group at all times.

In the 70s and 80s, Group Motion was part of the NEA Touring Program and was performing in Montana. We performed at a university and conducted a workshop as part of our residency. Eighty people filled the gym space. While we were working with different structures in smaller group division, the Crystallization got everyone involved at once. It was quite an amazing sight.

In one of the performances at the Gershman YMHA in Philadelphia, we invited the audience to join. We had about 200 people dancing, playing the Crystallization Game.

The Grid

From 3 to 40, depending on the space.
With or without music.

- Stand or sit at the periphery of the space. Sense the space and the people in it.

- Visualize the space as a grid consisting of right angles. Begin to travel and change your direction in right angles. No circles or diagonal lines.
- Start with walking, and later in the process, progress into variations of steps and ways of traveling, using levels, changes of speed, or by making contact.
- One can step out of the grid, and just observe at any time.

Variation

- Variations are endless and inspire ways of meeting, of traveling alone or together, observing oneself and each other.
- While stepping out, we observe and stay present in the dance of it. Observation supports skills of dynamics, of space and expression.
- You can invite the addition of diagonals or curves.
- Stepping out, or sitting out, may stimulate ideas for a dance, poem, or story.

Participants surrender to the Grid Dance, Friday Night Workshop, 2015 (photograph courtesy Bill Hebert).

Reflection

Brigitta—*Often in group improvisations, you'll see that dancers cluster together in the middle of the space, as if avoiding to venture out, and are intimidated to be see too much "out there." The Grid opens the space and makes room for a different kind of communication.*

The Grid allows for and encourages stepping out. It encourages traveling on your own. It allows for independence, yet a feeling of connectedness. Feeling safe, outstanding, or connected, whenever you are inspired. Stepping out allows dancers to make choices, choices about when and how to step out, and how and when to come back. As it suggests ways of traveling through space, we focus on spatial awareness, on inner and outer awareness. We sense the space all around us, behind, aside, and in front of us, above and below us. We practice peripheral vision. And we meet and connect with others from such perspectives. The Grid helps people get acquainted with each other on the dance floor at a group's first meeting. It is applicable for professional dancers, and for students of all levels of experience.

I forget who first introduced me to The Grid. It became one of Group Motion's favorite practices. Yet, years later, in 1999 when I studied and taught at Naropa University in Boulder, it was presented to me again by Barbara Dilley. Barbara, then interim director of the Naropa University dance program, was offering classes/workshops based on the Grid, rooted in her contemplative studies and experience. She spoke about maps in space and parallel corridors. She developed her own format that combined sitting meditation with writing, with eye practices, and spatial awareness.

Shadow Dance

For 5 to an undefined number of participants.
With or without music.

- The Shadow is another form of leading and following like a flock. Participants can follow leaders in any formation behind them, like a shadow. Those who shadow can change groups to follow another leader, or become leaders themselves at any time.
- Shadow formations can intersect and relate.
- One or several people follow one person in a line formation. Dancers may be moving slow, fast, or ecstatically at times, child-

Shadow Dance by students at University of the Arts, 2015 (photograph courtesy Bill Hebert).

like or celebratory at others. There maybe one or numerous lines forming, changing and transforming at the same time.
- The leading or following of each other changes, according to the initiative of each mover.
- Intensified expressions and communication may unfold into symbolism, mystical play, and ritual.
- The Shadow is really a form of following the leader, yet with an emphasis on spatial awareness, and the practice of the awareness of others. Sense the dancers behind you when you are leading, and tune into when you are following.

Reflection

Brigitta—*The structure is easy to understand yet it is also challenging. The challenge lies in the ability to take on a leading role, or to let go and surrender as you follow another.*

You will see lines of people in perfect synchronicity moving about the space in various ways of traveling. You will see a weaving through from place to place, and through each other's paths. Sudden turns of direction

Shadow Dance by participants of a Friday Night Workshop, 2015 (photograph courtesy Bill Hebert).

can change leadership instantly. Motions range from slow to high speed, sometimes with stillness, and then running, leaping, skipping, turning. From cautiously groping your way to ecstatic outbursts in circles, spirals, and other shapes throughout the space.

The Shadow Dance has evolved over time and years of practice. Some of the participants who have twenty or more years of this practice are able to perform this structure with the precision of choreography. You may see an in-the—moment piece no single choreographer could envision. The variety of patterns metamorphosing simultaneously, sometimes seem chaotic, sometimes in total harmony, appear like a field in nature. Expressions of a mythical nature are often seen and heard. It is not uncommon that voicing/chanting evolves within this dance.

As a musician and facilitator of this structure, looking in from the outside, I can see dynamic changes in the making. The "field" becomes transparent. I can see and anticipate decisions and support their progression. I may inject energy when necessary, or shift rhythm or texture to calm the process. For the most part, the music is a strong part of playing with this structure, yet without music, a keen sense of listening can be stimulated.

Frequently, the ecstatic nature of a Shadow Dance highlights the Friday Night Group Motion Workshop. It seems like a culmination of all the practices that have gone before it.

Exchange Game

For 10 to 20 participants.
With or without music.

- The group is divided in two, and forms two lines facing each other, at opposite ends of the room.
- One person steps out of the line and begins to improvise freely, eventually developing a repetitive movement.
- This person then starts to travel, taking the repetitive movement or phrase across the room, approaching a person on the other line.
- Now, in a brief mirror game, the movements are repeated in unison.
- The movers then exchange places with each other, and the second person will now improvise freely, taking the time to find their own authentic repetitive movement phrase, and then bring it to the opposite line.
- The game is continued in this manner, until the two lines have exchanged places.

Variations: Join In

- Everyone joins the movement of the approaching person when it becomes repetitive, and becomes still again when the new person leaves the line.

Join Ongoing

- Everyone in both lines moves, improvising on the given repetitive movement, continuing until the next person offers a new repetitive movement.

Tribal Exchange

- Two people begin, one from either side. Each person is accompanied with a vocal sound from the line they are approaching. The two people dialogue with each other through movement, as they meet and pass on their way across the floor.

Fast Exchange

- In this variation, one person quickly and directly crosses over to the other group, bringing a movement/sound to the new line.
- The line adapts to this movement, while one of the people in this line then crosses back to the first group, bringing a new movement to them.

Reflections

Manfred and Brigitta—*The original version of the Exchange Game was adopted from the Living Theater and has served as a seed for development of Group Motion games and structures. Although we observed the Living Theater's performance entitled,* Mysteries *at the Akademie der Kuenste in Berlin, Germany in 1965, that moment stays with us still.*

Moving or Being Still

For up to 30 participants.
With live music.

- Here everyone has the option of moving or being still, by himself or herself, or in relation to anyone, at any moment.
- This more open structure allows for multiple forms of engagements and interactions, almost like a free improvisation, but with the essential built in listening device of stillness.
- Live music is essential as the holder of time and space.

Reflection

Manfred—*The image of a fair or playground comes to mind, where people move around or sit, or stand still, participating in activity or watching, alone or in groups, initiating or following, being active or passive, talking, doing something, or listening, doing nothing. Everyone is part of the picture; everyone's presence affects the whole, even through just being there. The stillness is as powerful as the movement. It reminds me of a large group musical improvisation, where the pausing and listening of players can create space for the active music to define and articulate itself. Moving or Being Still frequently comes into play during the Friday Night Workshop process. It serves to generate and build a sense of the whole, while still*

Brigitta (*upper left*) guides workshop participants through Moving or Being Still, Friday Night Workshop 2015 (photograph courtesy Bill Hebert).

allowing for complete individual freedom and a multiplicity of choices of interplay. The key to coherence is the amount of listening, seeing, and sensing the larger picture.

Triangle/Diamond Dance

For any number of people in groups of 3.
With live music.

- Three people stand in a triangle formation, facing the same direction, at least an arm's length apart from each other
- The person at the front, or apex of the triangle, will be the first leader of the group. The leader must be aware of his/her own body.
- Like a flock of birds, as the leader turns, all of the followers turn, maintaining the triangle shape. Upon turning, the role of leader changes to the new apex of the triangle. The lead may be passed either to the left or right, slowly after several minutes, or quickly after leading for only a few seconds.

Students at University of the Arts practice the Triangle Dance 2015 (photograph courtesy Bill Hebert).

- If there are several triangles moving at the same time, they may intersect, passing over or through each other, but still should remain distinct from each other.

Variation: Diamond Dance

For any number of people in groups of 4.
With live music.

- Participants form groups of four, and move in a diamond formation, changing leading function with the change of direction.

Solo Variation

- At any time during the dance, one participant in the back of either the Triangle or Diamond formation may choose to break off and create a counterpoint solo to the unison movement of the group. S/he will return to the group whenever the solo feels complete.

Reflection

Manfred—*Like the flocking of birds when they travel in the change of seasons, in the arrow shaped or clustered formations that they create, usu-*

ally one bird at the tip of the flock leads. In the Triangle/Diamond Game, like the Shadow Game, a similar agreement and manifestation of trust is made and is at the heart of the dance. While we don't know by which mechanism the birds change their leadership, in this dance version the change is a provision of the agreement. When the leader changes direction and focus, the whole formation changes and brings another dancer into the lead, carrying on from where the previous leader has left off. This continuous exchange of leading and following has three empowering effects:

(1) One feels trusted as a leader to lead the whole group from your own impulse and movement intuition.
(2) One receives, absorbs, and experiences "learning," embodying the leader's movement as a follower.
(3) One experiences being a part of an extended group body, of a unit of three or four or more, moving through space, creating and shaping an internal space between each other, and an external space among the groups of bodies and their formations. Each is

Triangle Dance by students at University of the Arts, 2015 (photograph courtesy Bill Hebert).

traveling around, or even through each other, creating relationships of varying kinds, forming continuously changing physical, emotional, and energetic landscapes.

Group Motion started to work with the Triangle structure in the early Seventies. While the idea of "flocking" as an improvisational structure probably was in widespread use, Group Motion initiated this particular format of the Triangle.

The Triangle/Diamond Dance served as one of the structures that engaged a whole group of gymnasts at the same time, in Tokyo. The outcome was a fantastic, gigantic mosaic of contrapuntal movement of orchestral dimensions, including vertical formations. The gymnasts used the walls, and an endless variety of rhythms and dynamics, making a "large picture" out of the chaos of multiplicity.

Group Dialogue/Trialogue Dance

For 6 to 12 people.
With or without live music.

- As an expansion of the Dialogue structure, groups of two, three, or four dancers can move as one collective body or unit, and speak and listen to the collective bodies of two groups (Group Dialogue), or three groups (Group Trialogue), and engage in a "conversation" with them.
- The "speaking" of a group is generated by one person initiating a movement or movement/sound impulse, that is then picked up and played with. It is repeated in unison, or played with in a textural way, and woven into a collective statement by the whole group, while the other groups are "listening" in stillness, or in a subtle listening motion.
- Then another group "answers," creating their response collectively, until they become still.
- If there are three groups, the third group then takes over the "speaking" role.

Reflection

Manfred—*These group bodies exist with a spatiality and transparency like cell clusters or stellar systems, like galaxies. They have space within* them that can be intersected by another system, like galaxies in collision that are said to slice through each other without destructive effects. It is important to note that these "conversations" are held, not to win or lose, but to travel together in a form of collective dreaming, and in discovery of new territories of shared imagination and creation.

Another dramatic collision of two powerful entities happens in a famous play of the romantic era in German literature: Heinrich von Kleist's Penthesilea. Penthesilea is a Queen of the Amazons who finds herself in a battle with the Greeks, lead by one of their leading warriors, Achilles. These two larger than life characters clash in a fight between love and death, domination and surrender, a battle of the sexes of passion and power, mutual attraction, ending in mutual destruction. Their encounter rises to super human dimensions and proves to be almost impossible to be played by a single actor and actress. The idea of a dance of two group bodies seemed to me the only possible theatrical solution that could manifest the layering and complexity of the mythical dimension of this encounter. This idea, however, has yet to be realized. It may take an operatic format to do that.

Final Reflections on Space Forms

Brigitta—In her book, *The Language of Dance*, Mary Wigman writes:

> [It] is space which is the realm of the dancer's real activity, which belongs to him because he himself creates it. It is not the tangible, limited, and limiting space of concrete reality, but the imaginary, irrational space of the danced dimension, that space which can erase the boundaries of all corporality and can turn the gesture, flowing as it is, into an image of seemingly endlessness.... Height and depth, width and breadth, forward, sideward, and backward, the horizontal and the diagonal ... he experiences them in his own body ... through them he celebrates his union with space.

As a dancer, performer I reach though the space to the audience. It feels to me like invisible tentacles of various lengths transmitted by breath. I believe it is a dimension of sensibility that a dancer/performer can develop and by which s/he communicates. This is where projection comes into play, and may vary in strength depending on the ability to focus. We talk about stage presence, reaching through space, resonating with an audience.

Through thousands of workshops and with people of all ages, the youngest maybe 3 or 4, all negotiate and share the space without colliding, running into or hitting another. Somehow, magically, playfully, awareness expands, and sensibility grows.

Observing a small child running, rolling, crawling through space in between adult sized bodies that are moving in fast, slow and other various ways, there is a sense of weaving together, the weaving of an energetic field. Every thread and every spark of energy counts. It is like a gifting to one another, each participant adding to this morphing tapestry, raising awareness, inspiring one another in moving towards the next level. We used to call it moving towards bliss. I remember it was Joseph Campbell's phrase and it became our motto in the 70s and 80s. In the context of moving with a group and in close contact, you always had to find your next possible move, your next twist or turn towards 'bliss' or balance, towards wholeness. Being part of a group yet feeling the entirety of it, sensing it as an organism, it makes me think of how those dances are metaphoric for micro and macrocosmic events. The phrase "We are all one," becomes real. We can feel this organism, and at the same time be apart and keep our individuality.

I remember being five months pregnant moving with a group of dancers in a sculptural, Pilobolus-like fashion in our performance piece entitled *Crossing the Great Stream*. We were on tour in Germany, performing in Berlin. I managed to always be on top of this moving, morphing, transforming sculptural entity, being secure and protective and in balance with my pregnant body—no problem.

In the group space, we find balance through changes of dynamics, changes of highs and lows and of all the directions, and at times in stillness. Each of these Group Motion structures mentioned above have their own distinct spatial design or blueprint, a setting from which to embark and to come back to. They are holding a certain space that can be recognized. Each evolving pattern becomes recognizable by the observer. The audience will be able to participate, understand the rules, and follow the creative process.

In a Crystallization Dance, for example, we always imply a center, embodied by one person who initiates the crystal, not unlike a magnet that attracts. S/he offers the space for a group to gather in some form of a cluster. A cluster, we call crystal, whose shape varies greatly. It is building a space of its own, a space within the given space and from which to expand outward towards the periphery. Within such a pattern, there is room for a spectrum of expressions. Whether abstract or emotionally charged, the initiated impulse finds its movements and finds its form, spacing itself, spacing the body, and transforming the space. Qualities may be earth bound, grounded, others maybe ascending, reaching to the sky, so to speak. From a central initiation and shape, a space is formed sensing front and back and all around, multi-dimensional.

In a Grid Structure the group orients itself in the invisible rectangular grid space and its limiting orientation. The question emerges, how will these limitations affect the dancers? Moving into a space without circles, curves or diagonals turns out to offer another sense of freedom. It brings forth new possibilities of creation, influencing the expression and interaction of the dancers. Its particular functionality is motivating ways of relating and corresponding. Activities arise of intersection or parallel relation, distance and or closeness, solo or contact. The task of this particular spatial awareness with fewer dimensions, with or without music, challenges our basic ways of communicating. The Grid Dance offers a sense of spatial transparency. Observing a Grid Dance, the audience will be able follow easily in this visual and dynamic process their own spatial vocabulary.

The Areas Game is like an oasis, a refuge for any group of any age. Tell a group of 4 year olds to go into the space and be 'popcorn,' or explore the space of 'slime,' they will be delighted. And, with adults, there is no difference. For example, offer them the space of water from frozen to melting rain, and they too will be delighted. Our human adaptability thrives, our imagination dwells in those simple yet sensual kinesthetic conditions. As a group, we take in a wealth of nuances from each other's interpretations. Reinventing space, one's body space, the quality of space, transforming on the spot and in companionship can be so much fun, non-competitive, and non-threatening, reassuring to the body, mind, and spirit.

The Shadow Dance is amazingly empowering to anybody who finds her/himself as the leader of a queue while traveling through space. It is also wonderfully satisfying to be in such a queue as a follower. On a Friday Night whenever the Shadow Dance is announced, I have noticed a sense of relief, a sense of liberation. I believe the Shadow Dance structure it is a metaphor for democracy. As an outside observer, I can detect where the energy is about to evolve and which direction it will travel. A newcomer to the Shadow Dance may find her/himself surprised when being followed, realizing his/her responsibility of leading a group may cause moments of concern or disbelief. "Are they really following me?" At other times, a dancer may get carried away by the empowering task, not realizing when the energy is fading and when change is imminent, s/he may find her/himself crawling on the ground. The saying "In dance when you are up you are up and when you are down you are down" is manifested here in the blink of an eye. You can observe when somebody is using effort to maintain leadership. It will easily turn into chaos, until the next authentic leader emerges and a new order of ease and harmony is established. There is no bad space; all dimensions of space, of traveling, of speed and expressions are possible and valued. It is a tribal way of decision making, and of learning about "being at the right place at the right time." It generates spatial harmony, euphoria, joy, ecstasy, calmness, surrender, group consciousness, a tribal consciousness.

In the Exchange Game, we cross the space individually, while being seen and held by the group of dancers who stand in a line on opposite ends of the space. This setup is a chance for solo adventure. It is up to me, to make it fleeting or lasting; it is my time to command and transform the space. It is empowering to be the one who is crossing, traveling while the energy of a group is holding, supporting the space.

Sound

I was walking
The brimming sun was drinking my mind
Everything I saw was longing
The trees the field the sky
Even the pond that looked like an eye
Open in sleep
Then from a distance I heard the stream
I went I stood for long
Constant but ever moving
Light and emanating vibrations of deepest peace
The flowing water had no longing
In its form time and space
Music and dance were one
And through reflections of the sun
Infinity was shining
Later still and through the night
The stream kept on flowing inside

—Manfred

Time Dance

For 3 to 10 participants.
Without music.

- The group begins by sitting or standing, in any formation.
- One dancer initiates a basic time, a sound, a movement, a sound texture, or a sound based on words. Sound and movement go together and are repeated.
- The rest of the group joins this sound/movement until the entire group is in unison. This is called the "basic time," which becomes the background for solos.
- Then one person spontaneously breaks away. This dancer who breaks out of the "basic time" moves and sounds, improvising

freely. In doing so s/he is relating to this basic pattern, contrasting or harmonizing with it in any way. Eventually, s/he develops a repetitive sound/movement that will be adopted by the group as the new "basic time."
- The game continues as another person breaks out, and so forth.
- Participants must pay attention to the needs and abilities of the group. Their length of improvisation and relating will maintain the vitality. A new "basic time" can be energizing, or provide serenity and sustainability to the group.
- Through the basic time, the dancers can play, as they can change the movement/sound rhythmically, or spatially, and create different formations and relationships.

Reflection

Brigitta—*With solos, the breakaway to create a new "basic time" becomes like a jazz soloist playing against the theme continued by the group. The Time Game can be musically or theatrically oriented. Being*

Time Dance by students at University of the Arts, 2015 (photograph courtesy Bill Heber).

backed up by the basic time, for the solo player it is an opportunity to explore sound/movement spontaneously, and generate rhythmic and melodic ideas and phrases, as possible ingredients for choreography, or just for the fun of self-expression.

Message Dance

For 6 to 20 participants.
Without music.
The Message Game is a sound/movement structure played in a group context.
It is as much a musical structure as it is one for movement.

- The group is scattered, standing still, spread out randomly throughout the space, or in a specific formation.
- Starting from a place of stillness, one person will initiate a message of sound and movement.
- This may be just a grunt or a chuckle, or it could be a phrase using sound and movement. It is given spontaneously, and can be expressed once or repeated several times. Then this person is silent again.
- A second person now initiates a new message in response. Like a conversation, there may be moments of silence, or moments where more than one person is sending a message at the same time.

The conversation evolves as people concentrate on "listening" and "talking" to one another.

Variation: Rumor Game

- The message spreads like a rumor through the whole group, so that everyone repeats the message. The message can be repeated in unison, or at random. It will continue to be repeated until the energy fades. It may stop suddenly, or fade out gradually. New messages may overlap old ones.
- The Message Game can be played with all the dancers moving in slow motion. When a message is given, all dancers stop. And when the message ends, they continue to move again.

Reflection

Brigitta—*This game is an inspiring practice for listening, listening for nuances of expression and content. It can evolve into a heated "discussion," or a place of harmony, as voices and movements create a musical landscape of exchange. The base time is initiated by one person. It is held and repetitively developed into a sounding/moving landscape for the entire group. In this repetitive sound-dance, the participants relate playfully to one another. As they move, they can do so by being close together, or far apart. They can mirror the specific movement, or alter it. Yet the sound is the basis and stays the same throughout. The objective is for one person to ride on this basic sound, while s/he then breaks out of it. As if creating a contrast, or melodic counterpart to this existing base, s/he will play along in the most arbitrary, minimal, or contrasting way in relation to the basic time. S/he is the solo player, taking on a different texture, dynamic, and expression.*

The existing base time of the group serves like a drum beat that provides the timing for a flute or voice. It becomes the support system for the soloist. It can be a short interlude, or a longer one, but always ends with recognizable stillness. A new basic time will be established as a response. Again, the group will gradually, one by one, pick up on this new basic time, a new sound/movement. This game of sound/movement play can go on, changing spaces, relationships and dynamics of the group, accordingly with the subtle or powerful interplay of the soloist. The variations are endless.

When will someone break out? How will the basic time evolve? Like in a piece of music, its dynamic and form will take on its own life, depending on the energy of the group, their connection and ability to tune in with each other. Sensing the inner dynamic, the energetic trend, is an advanced skill. It requires keeping track of your own impulses and staying aware of the group. It requires transparency, an inner eye and yet openness to the whole. A sense of pleasure comes from surrender into the repetition and the group as a unit, a joyful freedom with the opportunity for totally letting go into one's own space as a soloist—being wild, outrageous, or quiet, meditative, funny, or acrobatically active.

Receiving Sound Energy

For any number of pairs.
With or without live music.

- Participants choose a partner: one person will be the giver and the other will be the receiver.
- The giving partner will send energy through voiced sound, as the passive partner responds through movement.
- With closed eyes, the receiving partner concentrates fully on listening, and responds to the quality of the voice, only if they feel moved to do so.
- The giving partner, with eyes open, observes the responses of the receiving partner, and aims to communicate a certain dynamic of energy via sound, rather than throw sounds to direct and manipulate. While voicing sounds, the giving partner can also move along with their own sounds.
- The receiving partner strives to embody the sound, rather than interpreting or reacting to the sound.

Variation

- Receiving Sound Energy can be played in a group of dancers, with one person sending energy to the group. The energy giver can remain active as s/he likes, and then become inactive, allowing another person to take the initiative to be the energy giver.
- This game can also be played as an interaction between participating dancers and musicians as a group.
- In another variation, each dancer follows a different musician or instrument.

Choreographic or compositional interplay will naturally occur between all of the dancers and all of the musicians.

Reflections

Manfred—*When the wind blows into the tree, the tree moves or dances according to the particular energy of the wind, be it gentle, strong, even, erratic, or stormy. When one throws something into a still water, be it a stone or a handful of sand, the water will move accordingly; it will ripple or splash. The energy of the sound maker in this game moves the still person accordingly, who lets herself/himself be moved, not from reacting to or interpreting the sound, but resonating with or becoming it. If they do not feel moved, they will not respond, just like the leaves of the tree remain still at times, when the wind does not reach them.*

The impact or the depth of experience on both sides depends on the depth of listening. The receiver will listen and let themselves be moved from a place of emptiness and non-anticipation. The giver will let the sounds or sequence of sound emerge and evolve from a place of listening to their own impulse and their perception of the receiver and his or her responses. The making of the sound does not want to be manipulative, disruptive, or violent, but a giving of energy in an organic way. It can take the form of a "song" or the "telling of a story," or be textural like the wind, in its different energetic manifestations.

It was discovered through scientific observation that when mothers talk or sing to their little babies, that the babies are responding with tiny movements to the rhythm and melodies of their mother's speech. (Condon and Sander, 1974). This became visible through film and the play back in super slow motion.

Jaclyn Carley, a Group Motion Company dancer, recalls:

> One day someone said, "When you are receiving energy, just feel like your whole body is a stretched skin on a drum, and that it comes at you, creates something out of you." Now before I dance, I just try to get into that feeling, my whole body being this taut, incredibly sensitive material. Even if a truck goes by outside, I get rattled when I am open to receiving energy that is in the air.

Conducting Sound Energy

For 2 or more, in pairs, or in groups of any size.
With or without live music.
The Conducting Energy Game is the reversal of the Receiving Energy Game.

- Played in pairs, one person becomes the conductor using movement. The other person responds with sound, translating the shape, volume, texture, and energy of the movement into the sound they "hear."
- The mover will conduct the movement from their intuition, and their body's impulses, and also with respect to the sound they "want to hear."
- For the group version, a group forms a circle, sitting cross-legged, or kneeling.
- One person enters the circle and begins moving.
- The group uses vocal sounds to mirror the person's movements, responding to the quality, volume, and intensity of the movement.

- The person in the center leads the sounds with his or her movements, similar to the way a conductor leads an orchestra.
- The central person moves as long as they feel to do so, and then rejoins the circle. Another may now enter the circle to conduct it.
- There may be more than one person moving inside the circle at the same time, in which case the members of the circle divide their attention among the different conductors.

Variation
- Conducting Sound Energy may also be played with a group of musicians.
- One person may conduct all the musicians and instruments with movement.
- A variation is for each participant to conduct a corresponding musician.
- Interplay can occur between all of the dancers and all of the musicians.

Reflection

Manfred—*These interactive communications of sound and movement mirror different phenomena of energy transference from one element to the other that can be found in nature. These elemental universal processes of communication from sound to movement and movement to sound get us in touch with layers of our physical, emotional, and energetic lives and memories. They can connect us back to the beginning of our own life in the stage of infancy, or of our human ancestor's primal existence, the time of life before words, when sound and movement were our primary languages.*

From a choreographic or compositional point of view, this energy transferal offers a very engaging and sensuous experience. The immediacy of the movement becoming sound and sound becoming movement provides the effects of making sense and offering surprise. It is particularly striking when one sound maker moves a group of moving receivers, and one observes the differences and similarity of the responses, or when one movement conductor triggers the sound making of a group of vocalizers or instrumentalists.

In our company's practice in the late Seventies, we created and performed a piece called Mitote, *in collaboration with the music group, "Musica Orbis," in which each dancer was linked to a musician, and his/her particular instrument. The moments of creation followed the alternating structure of Receiving and Conducting Energy; at one time the dancers were leading, and then the musicians led at another. The book, "The Teachings of Don Juan," by Carlos Castaneda, inspired the piece and in particular the passage describing a* Mitote *session, a spiritual shamanic practice in which each participating person connects with their partner in the spirit world. It was around the time of the making of this piece that these structures were created.*

Sound Activation/Soundscapes

For 5 to 8 participants.
With or without live music.

- A group of up to 8 dancers stands in a circle for a moment of stillness and listening.
- Then, one person, when ready, steps out and goes around the circle from one to the other, and after a moment of focusing, gives each person a sound or short sound phrase. This s/he repeats like a mantra, until it is received and put into movement by the receiver, who then continues to repeat the sound/movement phrase.
- The activator then goes to the next, and the next, until everyone has received a sound and is activated.
- The activated dancers then will break out of the circle and "play" with their sound/movement in space and time variations, and in interaction with each other.

Thus a soundscape is created, which then can also be directed and changed by the activator, who can stop and start the sound-movers at any time, until the whole group is stopped, and remains in stillness. Then, the activator chooses a new activator.

- The choice of sounds can be of rhythmic, melodic, textural, or verbal in nature, and can vary between the dancers. Or they can be rhythmic, melodic, textural and verbal within one activation.

Reflection

Manfred—*In all activation structures, a transmission of movement or sound from body to body, through touch or voice, from the activator to* the dancer or group is the *modus vivendi* and creates the playful, creative interactivity propelled by both expectation and surprise. Each act of activation is a kind of birth giving, an organic evolution from the seed of a shape into the growing of a dance. There is a lot of joyful discovery at work: how the realization of the given form or idea might, or might not, meet the intention of the activator. Or how, on the other end, the receiver experiences the kind of form or being they inspired the activator to shape them into, and where it takes them. It is also a great structure to facilitate movement invention, character formation, and the creation of instant choreography.

In this particular form of activation through sound, the focus is creating a composite of individual sounds and their embodiments into a landscape of a specific, yet varying nature. There is a particular beauty in the single mindedness of the sound embodiments and their interactive random coherence, like the soundscape of bird songs in a forest environment, or the simultaneous chatting of many voices in a party setting.

Words into Sounds

For any number of participants.
Without or without rhythmic accompaniment.

- Begin by standing still. Empty your mind as your instructor counts down from ten to one.
- At the end of the countdown, spontaneously choose and say a word. Repeat the word and begin to play with its sounds. Explore the timing and volume of the syllables, and the parts of the vowels and consonants.

For example:

OCEAN
OCH CH..CH..CH..CH..CH..CH
OCH..OCH..OOOOCH..OOOOCH..
OCH..NNNNNNNNNNNNNNNNNN
N.........O..N......O..N.....................O
OCHE...OCHE..OCHE...OCHE..OCHE

Let your body move with these sounds. Become a sounding, moving body.

Variation: Voice and Silence

- Stand in random order. Silently standing, focus on listening, observe your breathing.

- At random, begin to move and VOICE always when you move, be silent when you are still. Now reverse, VOICE only when you are still; move always when you don't voice.

Variation: Dialogue

- Listen and begin to communicate with other participants, creating a landscape of sound/movement dialogue, interaction, and exchange.
- Harmonize or contrast with each other's sound/movements.

Variation: Circle

- One person starts a sound movement.
- The next person adds to it, with another sound movement, until all are in, creating an instant harmonizing composition. Stay with it until you feel it has solidified and asks for change. Then, you reverse; the first person becomes silent and so on until all are silent again. Repeat as often as you like. Add a theme or specific topic.

Final Reflections on Sound Forms

Manfred—Before the verbal language came into play, the language of early humankind consisted of sound and movement. Likewise, in the early years of our personal human lives, the primary means of expression emerge from sound and movement. And even later in life, in our adolescent and adult stages, when we have full command of the verbal language, in certain intensified emotional or highly energized states, we revert to this primal way of expression. And we may and often do regard these expressions as raw or primitive, or out of control and inarticulate, but they seem to have necessity and irrefutable power.

While breath is the lifeline of our biological functioning, it is also ties in directly with our emotional life. We breathe according to how we feel. And vocal sound is an extension, of amplification of the breath. While it reaches deep into the subconscious memory of primal or earliest times of our existence and our inner life, it also communicates and connects and resonates with the outer world. Hissing sounds and their movement may recall wind or water or snake sounds, as well as evoke certain emotional states of being. This sound language brings us closer to the animal life and the elements, like the waves of the ocean or the running of rain, the crackling of fire or explosions of thunder. Clicking, or clapping, or stamping sounds, can carry audible body rhythms without drums that also resonate with both inner and outer realities. Sounds reach the ears everywhere, even when the eyes cannot "see" their sources. A group that moves and sounds together can create a connectivity between its body/sound/dancers that is unique, and reaches across many layers of conscious and subconscious realms of collective memory and imagination.

The direct alignment of the sound with the movement provides articulation or differentiation and reminds of the coordination of the conductor's movement with the movements and the sounds of the orchestra. The "letting go" aspect of sound making and moving has a liberating effect of releasing, asserting and communicating holistically, and is instantly healing and energizing. We have bodies to move and we have voices to sing, and the integration of the two provides a powerful larger than life capacity.

When I introduce sound/movement practices to my dance students at the University of the Arts, my teaching ground for over forty years, they break into an aliveness, a mode of having fun, to a degree that they rarely display otherwise. It is a huge discovery that they have a voice to dance with because they are mostly taught to be quiet and keep their lips tight. In dance, at least in the white, Western culture of dance such as ballet, jazz, modern dance, vocal sound is very rarely applied, while it is common in tribal or ethnic dance, as well as folk theater and martial arts. Group Motion started to integrate sound in 1967 with the multimedia dance work *Countdown for Orpheus*, and it has become an experimental practice in postmodern performance, most notably in the works of Meredith Monk.

In the Conducting Sound Energy structure, where one dancer steps into the circle of sound makers, evoking sound responses through her/his spontaneous movement impulses, the energy and intensity of the dance goes up several levels, as if the sound is amplified. It is a magical experience of energy transfer from one medium to another. This transfer has a more intimate quality in the one-on-one version, one dancer being echoed, read, translated into sound by the other. The two roles of being initiator or receiver will always find themselves being reversed during the course of the dance, creating an experience of being seen and sounded. And in the reverse structure of Receiving Sound Energy, the experience of letting oneself being moved by the sound maker puts the mover into a trance like state of listening and receiving and becoming the sound, like being "birthed" by the voice of the other. In the process of energy transference from one sounder to a group of movers who have their eyes closed, one will see a striking form of organic and synergistic choreography of sameness and difference.

The potentiality of the interfaces between movement and sound enters a new dimension with the invention of new technologies. (See Part II Group Motion Practices: "Practice of Interaction with Technology"). Ultrasonic beams can triggers the sounds of a keyboard, or iPods attached to the bodies of dancers can carry the music with them into the larger space, or miked and amplified floors and sets activated by the dancers' movements can create the soundscapes for the performance. From the mother's talking and singing to the infant's tiny dances, to the primal scream and other sound therapies, from artistic renderings of sound/movement interchanges to the sonar detections of movements from the depth of the ocean or from distant galaxies, sound and movement synthesis is one of the most powerful forms of communication in the micro/macro universe.

One of my favorite Sound Dance structures is Sound Activation or Soundscapes. This dance of triggered and activated sound/movements makes me think what we might see if we could look inside a brain and could see the singular life of neurons and their simultaneous existences in a web of interactions, creating larger projections of ideas or images from their overlapping singularities. There is a particular pleasure in embodying this single minded, or should we say double minded way of being, in its variances and its connections to others. In my experience of doing it and seeing others engage with it, this repetitive, sound movement action does not get boring or tiring, but gains energy as it goes on, ecstatically.

WORD

Not different
But differently after all
Are words
Speaking
When sounds and impulses of movement
Click into the system
Hammer in rhythms the codes of tones
Move to decipher the text of dream

Movement is an essential form of human knowledge and interaction,
Like math, science, and language.
As no one would say, "I don't speak,"
It is not possible to say,
"I don't move. I don't dance."

—Manfred

Traveling Landscapes

For 5 to 20 dancers.
With or without music.

- The group gathers at one end of the space.
- The path of traveling will be determined at the outset. It may be all across the space, going back and forth, just a few feet in one direction, or circling clockwise or counter clockwise.
- The objective of this structure is to create and build together, based on a theme that is given by one of the participants.
- Each beginning is made evident by the calling out of the theme, while the ending is signaled by coming to stillness.
- If live music is part of the event, the ending can be signaled by a distinct musical cue, or by the fading of the music.

This structure requires advanced improvisational skills: the ability to translate a theme, to visualize the theme as a dance, a movement quality, a texture, individually and in context of the group. The theme may be an idea, an image, or a sentence. For example: "rain," "doors everywhere," "ocean," "city street." The theme must be clearly stated and repeated. Each theme offers the opportunity to enter into a journey together. Each dancer may transform him/herself in his/her own way, or by relating to another. The group can form the image with a mosaic of actions, or become the image through a shared movement or movement quality.

For example, OCEAN:

I may start a movement and sound that will be joined by others. As I create an ebb and flow of wave-movement into a dance, one person in the group may decide to be a swimmer in the ocean, and find her place within the waves of the group. A story of sorts may unfold, and find its ending as the swimmer lands at the shore, or becomes her own wave.

Or, STORM:

One part of the group may create the dynamic, speed, texture while others may be moved by the storm and find a form, or state of being, within it. It may end when the storm is calm, breaks the entire landscape, or freezes into an image. Environmental themes lend themselves well to this structure.

Reflection

Brigitta—I am reminded of a wheel of life. You never know what to expect next. As you are in it, you can't escape. You find your place, either leading or following. Traveling Landscapes has a micro/macro cosmic dimension, forming and transforming itself anew for an extended period of time. Traveling Landscapes is about decision-making and active imagination. The choosing and interpretation of themes will determine the journey of this dance. It lends itself well as a performance score and for choreographic initiation or exploration.

The Traveling Landscapes structure can be adopted and played by participants with various levels of experience, such as professionally engaged dancers, non-professional movers, intergenerational dancers, and by children and teens. Some decisions can be made before the start; others may be made at the spur of the moment.

On a physical level, this structure is about choosing a spatial path at the outset of the game. Depending on the size of the space, the size and experience of a group, and the anticipated goal, the group of dancers may be asked to travel from one side of the space to the other. In this arrangement the arrival on one end of the space will indicate the beginning or the end of each development of a theme. Other spatial options of traveling can be a circle or a spiral, starting at the periphery leading to the center, or reversed, starting from the center and moving towards the outer edge.

Beyond the play and practice, the goal could be a performance, which provides the additional dimension of being witnessed, heightening the awareness of the participants. It will deepen the sense of perception and organization, while intensifying the meaning of the message. No matter its spatial setup, Traveling Landscapes is a "by chance" process because of its emphasis on the choice of themes.

It is the realization of each theme, their collective embodiment, which determines the process for the entirety of the dance-journey. At the end of each interpretation of a theme, and the arrival at their respective spaces, the dancers maintain a moment of stillness. As the stillness is held in the last position of each dancer's movement, it reveals a final image of the theme and allows the dancers to stay with the imprint of their experience. After about 30 seconds of pause, the next theme will be announced. Themes maybe spontaneously announced by the participating dancers, or prede-

Participants form Traveling Landscapes, Community Performance Project, 2009 (photograph courtesy Colin Harvey).

termined beforehand in writing. Writing themes beforehand is also a wonderful chance to involve an audience.

For example:

Each participant writes a theme on a piece of paper that is folded up and put into a hat or basket, and in completion of this process each dancer will also pick one of those pieces, reading it silently. If each reader is a dancer, you put it back if you get your own. Or members of the audience write their ideas/themes on a given piece of paper that is collected in a container and presented to the dancers for drawing. The dancers may read those before the journey begins or read and call out during the process. Who is next to call out the theme whether by chance or predetermination becomes part of the piece.

What are the implications of a theme, what does it offer in regard to spatial arrangement, to timing, texture, rhythm, shape, or physical contact? Its mosaic organization of ideas, of movement elements and of music, and of sound making or verbal expression motivates the formation of a group, their interaction and relationship to each other.

In this shared collaborative creation of a Traveling Landscape dance, the participants align in an abundance of emotional sensations as each theme reflects one participant's ideas linked to personal or otherwise inspired motivations or impulses. "Trees," "water," "miracles," "drought," "storm," "isolation," "migration," the themes may trigger deeply felt impulses or states of mind, and indicate a sense of play, of spectacle, of crisis, or otherwise felt sensations which offer and determine the movement quality, texture, sounds, or a movement motive which influences the dynamic progression of the journey.

On the spiritual level, we can recognize the authenticity of such impulses and in the process of their development, that the dancers encounter unexpected, surprising abilities to take action, to create movement, to assert power, and experience transformation. On this level, a sense of timelessness and effortlessness maybe experienced by the participants and by the observer. In this intuitive state of dance/movement/sound improvisation, the dancers activate the process of embodiment, of formulating expression, diving into the realm of the unknown, the unspeakable and unforeseeable.

Say What You Do

    For 4 or more dancers.
    With or without music.

- Spread out in the space. All participants will begin to move independently of each other. The choices of the motions are spontaneous, without any particular design or agenda.
- The movers observe their movements and describe them audibly, as if they are reporting to an outside world that cannot see them—reporting their positions, the intensity or quality of their movements, describing what is happening to his/her body, its relation to the space, and to the other participants.
- The movement speed, energy, and rhythm may be reflected in the way they speak or voice their actions. The movers may shift to include comments about how they feel, or how someone else's presence affects them.
- This "self programming" will have the movement principally in the leading role, and in the speaking in the following function, but the roles may shift, or become simultaneous.
- At some point, the facilitator may bring the process into a hold, and ask just one of the participants to continue while all the others are pausing and listening. Then after a while, everyone is asked to resume their action until another person, or two people simultaneously, are called out...

Variation
- Intermittently, or in a separate round, the process may be done in slow motion, in both the moving and the speaking.

Reflection

Manfred—*This word dance of self-observation lives in the interface of movement impulse and spoken word cognition, or right brain/left brain intersection, and is a journey of playful self-discovery. It is to be noted that in spite of the seeming randomness, the movement progressions always come from some internal need, or some external triggering caused by perceptions of other people's movements and sounds. Nothing is ever accidental here. From a bird's eye view, one would see the emergence of an interesting coherence or narrative, in each of the player's pathways.*

Word/Movement Mirror

For 2 players.
With or without live music.

This structure is an adaptation of the Conducting Energy structure, where the "mover" conducts the "sounder," who translates or mirrors the movement with sound.

- In this version, the mover conducts a verbal response of the verbalizer who translates, mirrors, or associates the movement in the moment, with words.
- Translations can be literal, or nonliteral, linear, or nonlinear.
- Sounds and words can both be interspersed in the following of the mover.

Variation

In this version, four people can play in a dialogue format.

Two movers and their associated verbalizers take turns in moving/talking and thus conduct a conversation with each other.

Sounds or words can both be applied.

Chat Room

For 3 players.

The Chat Room Host, The Voice of the Chat Room Host, and The Visitor.

With or without live music.

If live music is used, it is recommended that the verbalizers are amplified.

- The Chat Room Host is the dancer/mover and occupies the stage space.
- The Chat Room Host Voice is a speaker seated on the stage left sideline, facing the Host.
- The Visitor is a speaker seated down stage front, and slightly stage right, facing the Host.
- The Visitor observes and begins to engage the Host, asking questions, and or commenting on the movement, in an attempt to make connection, or communicate with him/her.
- The Host dancer/mover "responds" in movement, while the Visitor is verbally responded to by the Voice of the Host.
- The Host dancer/mover serves as the focus of the conversation, with his/her movements being the point of reference, or filter, or medium, for both the speech of the Visitor and the Voice of the Host. The Voice of the host may also use sound.

- It is essential that the verbal conversation is not a direct line of interaction in direct response to the words of the other speaker, but that it always goes through, or is filtered, or triggered by the movement statements, or movement initiations of the Host.

Variation

- A theme, such as "summer," "sex," "aliens," " dance," etc., can be chosen to become the "topic" of the conversation.
- In public performance settings, the themes can be solicited from the audience.

Reflection

Manfred—*These juxtapositions of movement and word play, with literal and indirect layers of movement languages, along with their verbal perceptions, interpretations, and associations explore the interactive space between word and movement generation and expression.*

Writing Process and Activation

For 4 to 20 players in three phases.
With or without live music.
With paper and pen.

Phase One:

- The facilitator asks each participant to write down five words, referring to a collectively shared theme or image, and numbers each word, one to five. If desired, larger numbers can be used, but 5, 6, or 7 words work best for this structure. Let us examine five.
- People are then asked to turn over the page and to write down a random new order of the numbers between one and five: 3,1,4,5,2 for example, and then attach the respective words to the new order of numbers.
- From this new order, each participant is asked to write a poem/paragraph/text, connecting the words, with the potential addition of new words. Keep following the progression of the new order.
- The paper will be folded and placed anonymously into a "hat," from which each player will then draw a piece of paper, other

than one's own. Each player now has a poem/text of someone else in the group.

Phase Two:
- The facilitator will then ask the players, one at a time, to select a group of dancers from the participants and place them, one at a time, physically into a shape/form/sculptural position in the space. They form a tableaux, image, or landscape of however many bodies they choose, referring to the poem created as the beginning set up for the dance.

Phase Three:
- The activator/choreographer will then read the poem/text out loud, preferably through a microphone, while the dancers hold their positions.
- With a second reading, which can be delivered creatively with verbal and sound animation, even with singing and live music, the dancers will begin to move from where there are, following their own impulses of movement, in relation to the words, the tableaux form, and the physical and spatial relationship of the other dancers.

This spontaneous, authentic, individual and collective response may be nonlinear, nonliteral, or not following or acting out the reading. The movement is in interaction with the reading and with the group on a movement plane.

- Each participant will have their turn to activate a group from the poem received.

Reflection

Manfred—*The duality of verbal and nonverbal consciousness offers its own interplay here. The parallel universes of the word language and its literal and metaphoric meanings and understandings on the one hand, and the movement language with its sense perception, kinesthetic body language, and associative images on the other, illuminate each other in a larger space of co-existence and interactivity. While this complexity is actually at work at all times of our waking life, we are usually not conscious of it, and operate only on one or two levels of awareness. The word/ movement games playfully lift the curtains from the different layers, and let us experience the whole, a large space, a kind of super-consciousness.*

The collectivity of the process, the giving over of one's writing to the choreographic vision of someone else, and the intuitive movement embodiment of the group is an inspiring and liberating experience.

Textography

For 4 to 12 players.

This structure provides a combination of improvisational performance and choreographic practice. The number of participants is equally divided into pairs of "performers" and "choreographers."

- Each pair communicates via cell phone texting. The performers on the stage space are wearing their phones attached with rubber bands to their wrists, while their respective choreographer/partners are positioned in the audience, or observer space, and use their devices to text their respective performers/partners.
- The process begins with the choreographer's texting instructions to their performer. The text receiving signal will alert the performer and s/he will then put the instructions into action, realizing them in their own understanding and interpretation, and continuing to play until a new instruction is given, and so on.
- The choreographic directions are given independently but simultaneously to the respective performer partners, so there might be two, or three, or four performers on the stage playing out their individual text directives at the same time. These directives may consist of movements, actions, sounds and words and can also be given and realized in interaction with other performers, and the overall choreographic or theatrical space.
- The play will go on until each of the performers has been directed to either stop and be still, or to exit the stage space.

Live improvised music, potentially but not necessarily played by the same number of musicians linked individually to the number of performers, will support and interact with the stage space, and can be part of the collective creation. It can also be decided to give the process the focus on an overarching shared theme.

Variation I
- In a variation with a greater choreographic emphasis, one choreographer gives the instructions to *each* of the performers individually, thus having more control over the whole of the movement. There can also be two directors, each controlling/instructing a group of performers.
- Again, live music and or a chosen theme can support the process.

Variation II
- In this more extreme experimental variation, the choreographers are in a different and separate space from their performers and each other, without being able to see them. Their only connection to the stage space could be via Skype.
- The choreographers, as well as the performers, will make their choreographic choices in relation to the music. The process will continue for the duration of the music. It can be videotaped and played back to all participants at the end.

Variation III
- In a performance setting, members of the audience can be invited to become the choreographers and be linked to respective performer partners. In this set up, there can also be an agreed upon thematic focus such as "supermarket," or "beach time," etc.

The Textography structure applies itself best in the context of dance or theater composition or improvisation classes, company rehearsals, and live performances. An important aspect of the application in class or rehearsal settings will be the analysis and discussion of the process, including any replay of the video documentation.

Reflection

Manfred—*Textography is a newly created Group Motion structure. It lives in an interface with a technology that has become a constant extension of our bodies in daily life. The messaging reality is almost like a parallel universe of connectedness that is hidden. In the space of Textography, this "universe" is exposed as an interconnected reality, becoming conscious while still also following subconscious impulses on both ends of the action. The dimensions of individual and collective creation are playfully and spontaneously interwoven in mysterious and nonlinear ways. It is to be remem-*

bered that nothing is truly random or accidental, and everything is interconnected in the larger space. In a way it reminds us of space travel and the relationship and dialogues between the astronauts and ground control stations, of the technological dream world of creative videogames.

Storytelling Dance

For up to 12 participants.
With live music.
This structure lives in the interactive space between words, movement, and music.

- It starts from a movement meditation: a Grid Dance, a Moving and Being Still Dance, or a Doing Nothing Dance, with everyone in the dance space.
- When one of the players feels inspired, s/he will step out and take the "story telling place," preferably at a microphone.
- S/he will then let a real life memory, or a remembered dream, or an in the moment imagined story come into consciousness, and begin to verbalize it in whatever mode he or she chooses. It can be plain speaking, or speaking with sounds, or singing.
- The movers/dancers in the dance space will receive the story from where they are, with their bodies and minds and from their emotional/energetic states of being, and begin to move. Each will move from this reception, being with, resonating with, and manifesting the flow of the narration in whatever form it comes to them, similar to the Receiving Sound Energy dance.

It is not the objective to mime or act out the story, but to translate, transfer it into a kinesthetic response. That responsiveness may include interaction with other dancers. It is important to note that stillness or no response, when it comes from an authentic place, is a valid option.

- The live music is an equal partner in this process. Silence when needed, listening to both the spoken words and the movements, and transparency in the playing, are all essential elements of creating this space.

When the narration of the story is completed, the narrator will step back into the dance space, where the movement meditation will resume, until the next storyteller emerges.

Reflection

Manfred—This structure can be understood as a variation or extension of the Receiving Energy Game, where one person is moving the group of movers by his/her sound making, or music playing. Here, the sound maker is using words in the telling of a story or a dream. The movers are finding their movement responses in their body, in resonance with both the form (sound, dynamics, and rhythm), and the content (image, emotion, meaning) of the words and the narration. It is a striking, illuminating spectacle of transmission or translation between the different media: the spoken word, the dance, and the music.

Alter Ego Monologue

For 2 Players.
See size variations below.

- One of the two players delivers a monologue they have memorized.
- The other player moves/acts as their alter ego, embodying and expressing their own version with movements, sounds, or even words. The alter ego can play with thoughts or emotions, dual or multiple personality traits, or the shadow self of the speaking ego. This movement alter ego can be manifested theatrically or abstractly, physically close, even connected, or spatially apart and can change modes.

Variation I

- The movement score is designed and composed after improvisational experimentation, and follows a set direction of interaction and relationship.

Variation II

- The spoken monologue is improvised and created in the moment.
- The two players can alternate the role roles of speaking or moving.

Alter Ego Dialogue

For 4 or 6 players.
With or without live music.

- Pairs of players (two or three) are engaging in a set scene of two or three characters,
with each player having an alter ego partner.
- The additional feature of the scene structure is that the alter egos can interact and relate with each other, independent of their egos. Their way of playing is improvised, while the egos are following a set script. Their action and speech choices, however, are made in the moment and in interplay with their alter egos, as well as with their scene partners.

Variation I

- After improvisational experimentation, the ways of interaction with their egos and between the alter egos are designed and set.

Variation II

- Each of the ego players may have up to three alter egos.

Variation III

- In this variation, the alter ego scene is purely a movement event.
- The interaction between the egos and their (potentially even physically) attached alter egos is happening in a silent or music supported space, and exists in the dimension of abstract movement invention and dance.

Reflection

Manfred—The alter ego concept exists in varying forms: the shadow self, split or multiple personality or dissociate identity disorder, the avatar, the doppelgänger, spirit doubles, evil twins, trusted friend, in literature, film, folktale and myth. Think of Dr. Jekyll and Mr. Hyde, Superman and Clark Kent, Gregor Samsa and his cockroach.

We all know it in the form of the inner voice that contradicts, disapproves or encourages or advises the actions or words of our foreground ego-side of self. In experimental movement theater described above, the alter ego scene structure takes this concept to a different more playful, symbolic level, where the embodiment of both sides is exposed simultaneously and in apparent interaction. It creates interesting theatrical spaces and opportunities using the effect of "Verfremdung," as in Berthold Brecht's Epic Theater, where transparency and exposure of multiple layers of the characters or the script emerge.

At the Theater Department of the University of the Arts, I once directed

Sartre's play "No Exit," in which three characters find themselves in their after lives in "hell," a hotel room from which there is no escape. I staged this very wordy play, with its famous line from one of the characters: "Hell is other people," with the concept that during the course of the play each of the characters finds themselves multiplied in the form of three alter egos, nine altogether. They were moving, shadowing, echoing, interfering, amplifying the dialogue of the three Egos, exposing different layers of their past and present personalities, and ending with the somewhat accepting realization, " So here we are forever." "Let's get on with it."

Final Reflections on Word Forms

Manfred—We often find that dance and movement speak what words cannot say. The reverse seems also true. Both are languages in their own right. What happens when they join, move, and dance together? What goes on in the space between? I often wonder about the life of words in dreams. They are sparse and hard to remember, but sometimes I have found myself speaking out loud, and with that, of course, waking myself up and losing the dream. This does not seem to happen the same way with movement in dreams. We actually get up and sleep walk at times and then go back to bed without waking. Movement and images seem to be the primary language in the subconscious world, but when words come in they often carry a certain significance.

Hearing voices of God or the Gods in dreams, or even in some rare waking states, seems to have been something more commonly experienced in the pre-literary ages, before the written word became dominant, before the break down of the bi-cameral mind. In the strange and dramatic transition from the oral to the literary age, we find, for instance in the Ancient Greek culture, the fascinating phenomenon of oracles, the eremitic people living in caves speaking in tongues, predicting the outcome of wars or other future events, in a form of gibberish that channeled the lost voices of the Gods that had vanished from peoples' inner ears, only to be maintained by schizophrenics and other entranced people.

Under the influence of mescaline and being naked out on a meadow some time in the early Seventies, when the Group Motion Dance Company spent some weeks in the woods of upstate New York, working on a dance piece based on Carlos Castaneda's *The Teachings of Don Juan*, I found myself rendering a cryptic verbal statement that I would most likely not have made otherwise. I remember saying with a sense of a revelation, "The flower is a printed circuit." While logistically seemingly nonsensical, it made a poetic and mystical sense to me. In the poems of surrealists like Rimbaud those kinds of crossings and meldings of worlds in their nonlinear, contradicting ways are powerful pathways to insight and resonance with a larger scope of visionary consciousness. It was Arthur Rimbaud, in my mind one of the most visionary poets of all times, who wrote in his *Illuminations*: "A universal language will come," an oracle to decipher he left to everyone thereafter.

Dance of course, is often called a universal language, but that is more of a 21st century perspective, which is not to say that it was not in Rimbaud's visionary purview. From my perspective, and in the context of the investigation of the significance of "Word Dances," this universal language the poet might have been envisioning could be one of speaking and moving at the same time, as described in the Say What You Do Dance, in which there is a superimposition of verbal and movement streams of consciousness.

Spoken Word and Rap seem to hint at that kind of an understanding, however the element of movement is still embryonic. We have seen a different balance of moving and speaking trace back from the dances and choruses of Greek Tragedy, through postmodern dance and performance art experimental versions. Some of those renderings remind of the sound/word/dance of Eurythmy, a spiritual practice developed by the philosopher, educator Rudolph Steiner. (Steiner, 1924) In most of these forms, however, there seems to be a primary and secondary function of the word and the movement, meaning that one is either accompanying and supporting or dominating and overshadowing the other.

In my experience of the Group Motion practices of Word Dances, the most potent, and still not fully realized relationship between the two languages, is one of shared independence and relatedness at the same time, a nonliteral, non-interpretive dialogue, an equal partnership that appears to be almost incidental, almost ignoring the other and yet both manifesting a simultaneous reality. In one of my more theater related word/movement practices, I ask the performer to speak a monologue or a stream of consciousness passage while moving rapidly and completely from purely bodily impulse, one that is not functionally related to the word content or sensical at all. This practice can provide surprising and totally unpredictable results, becoming a drawing board for an exciting, new and refreshing way of creating character study.

This process is somewhat reminiscent of Merce Cunningham and John Cage's approach in creating music/dance collaborations as independent actions governed by chance. But of course, with Cunningham and Cage, it manifests through the combined efforts of two creators in the process of creation separately and apart from each other, only to come together in the performance. And with reference and reverence to that form of collaborative creation, I want to emphasize the fact that the speaking and moving at the same time format in the embodiment of a single person is only one part of the spectrum of Word Dance.

In the Solo Dance Writing Game structure, the co-creative potency of this process again is fueled by the duality of dependence and interdependence that is at work, the coincidental and yet non-coincidental relationship between the nonverbal and the verbal expressions that are woven together, drawing from both the conscious and the subconscious sources of the performers. With live improvised music, these poem/dances provide a delightful insight into each person's perception and their associative resonances, and give the outside observers their own space of reflection.

The in-between space of all of the components is both, meditative and playful, and can provide a mystical experience of collective sub/consciousness, a kind of super-consciousness that does not need an explanation or interpretation. I wrote poetry starting in high school, way before I discovered dance, while I had practiced music throughout my early childhood and teenage years. What connected all three languages most notably was the element of rhythm. Also, in early years starting at age six or seven, I found myself drawn to storytelling, often in front of my classmates before the teacher came in. I was re-telling stories that I had picked up in the Christian Youth group, acting them out at the same time with movement. One of my favorite "acts" was playing the reporter of a soccer game, also acting out my report with movement. While I sometimes think of soccer playing as my first dance experience, these story telling events were more like my first theater. Of course, this was again, a single person word/movement practice.

In the Storytelling Dance, which divides the function of wording and moving between single story teller and the moving group, it is essential, as it is in all of the word /movement structures, that they are in the moment creations or improvisations with some potential aspects of remembering or re-creation. Equally important is that they are not interpretations or illustrations of each another, but that they travel on the path of their own intuition while creating this dual reality from listening, observing and following their impulses. It should be noted that the telling of the story may take on musical elements like rhythm and melody or "Sprechstimme" an expressionist technique between speaking and singing, and that the dance is free to use stillness, or speed changes, or any form of interactive or contrapuntal dynamics or movement expression. This indirect or abstract relationship opens doors and windows of imagination and perception.

Once, in a practice session, I was asked to tell a story. While I went to take the microphone I had a certain story in mind. As soon as I got there, that changed: a childhood memory popped into my mind, one that I picked up from my mother telling me. It was the story about being at a kindergarten in Africa about three years old, when one day the building caught on fire while I was outside at the time. The fire burnt fast, and for some reason, I tried to run into the fire, being held back at the last minute by a grown-up. Eleven children died. When I started to tell the story I came to the point of saying that there were children inside not being able to get out ... the group on the dance floor became very still and hardly moved. At that point I had to stop.... I could not go on talking. I believe we ended the whole process. The past had become a presence that I could not bear. The embodiment of the words had attained an overwhelming power through the paradoxical stillness of the dance. This re-experience of a moment that I did not even remember myself, but only knew from my mother telling me, could only happen for me in the space between the dance and the word, a dance that was embodied, not acted out, along with the words that rose up in the moment of speaking.

Ritual

I pray
That I be awake at dawn
Stand in the doorway of each breaking day
Feel the wind
Let myself be moved
Like a blade of grass
Like a drop of water in the stream
Walk on the beach of the morning without desire
Watch my footsteps be printed and washed away
Open my mouth not to talk but to sing
Speak with my whole being
Soul heart brain muscles bone and skin
That I be what I am
Without question or doubt
Like a plant or a bird or a stone
Give what I have to give and when
Like the fruit tree that renders its fruit when it has to
Step out into the street with joy
Let me movements flow with everyone's movements
Let my body touch another body with love
Do not hold on
Be free of concepts past present and future
Be moved to move breath by breath
Let my life be danced by grace
Let my life be dance

—Manfred

House or Village Square Dance

For 5 to 12 participants.
With live music.

- In a large and open dance space, the participants will draw with masking tape, the boundary of their own personal space, as if to

mark the ground plan of their imaginary house in an imaginary village square.
- The space in the center remains open and serves as public space.
- At the start of the ritual, each dancer occupies his/her own house and manifests a mode of being. It may be a movement phrase, a quality of moving, or a movement with sound or words, a mantra of their own personal way of being "at home." This mode should be continuous, or repetitive, and identifiable in its specificity.
- At any given moment, any of the dancers may decide to go out, to leave their home space, and move through the open public space, and visit someone in their home, talking in the mode of being with the host and playing within that space. There can be several visitors at once. However, when the host decides to leave, the visitors also have to leave. Likewise, no one can enter someone's house when no one is there.
- In the public space, or "village square," people can meet and move and play in any way, being still, or moving by themselves, or in relationship to others.
- When they decide to go back home, they may take up either the previous signature movement, or develop a new one.
- The dance may end when everyone decides to stay out in the public space.

Variation
- One of the four sides or corners of the space can be marked and dedicated as a verbal/story telling area into which individuals or groups enter at times of his/her own choosing and engage in word play for as long as s/he feels verbally motivated. Movement, stillness, or sound can accompany the free form verbalizations.
- The Houses or Village Square Dance can also be played in a natural environment like a beach, or in a forest clearing or park, where each person chooses a particular space in the environment, and creates their own ritual within it that invites others to visit and join.
- These rituals may use objects, or play with elements of the environment: trees, sand, rocks, grass, or water of the natural habitat. There is also a dedicated open space where all dancers can

meet in play, creating landscapes of movement or stillness within the landscape of the environment.

Reflection

Manfred—*The Houses or Village Square Dance celebrates the co-existence and balance between the individual/personal and the communal/public space. Played at its highest level of awareness and sensitivity towards both aspects, it can provide for a very rich and layered experience of time and space interplay. The seemingly chaotic nature, when seen from a larger perspective, reveals coherence and structure of an unexpected, and organic order.*

Group Motion has played this ritual in such different and diverse spaces as a large church in Bermuda, beaches in Maine, the Great Sand Dunes in Colorado, red rock desert spaces outside Sedona, and an outdoor amphitheater space at Arcosanti, Arizona.

Object Dance

For 6–12 players.
With live music.

At the start of the dance, the players are asked to take some time to search for an object to move and dance with. They are asked to do this from a place of "emptiness," making their search without pre-meditation, or agenda, choosing their object without judgment, letting whatever calls their attention be okay, regardless of how big or small, beautiful or ugly, natural or synthetic, old or new the object might be. If the dance is happening in the context of a retreat, or a weeklong workshop, the process of searching might be given two days time and might include the natural environment as source. After the completion of the search, each player will bring his/her object into the practice space. They will be asked to find their spot, and allow for some time to meditate on the object before they start moving with it, or in relationship to it. Listening to their body, they will begin to move in any way that they feel like moving, regardless of the object's normal function or purpose.

- The object can become an extension of the body, or serve as a "mask" for a movement character. The modalities of object integration and relationship can vary and change. In the process of

Brigitta Herrmann, performing *Walking Piano* by Remo Saracini, 1987 (photograph courtesy Margie Politzer).

exploration s/he will discover certain images or movement progressions that want to be remembered, or put into a sequence that can be repeated and made into a ritual dance.
- After sufficient time, the facilitator of the exploratory process will call one or two of the participants to perform their dance while the others are observing, and then ask everyone to go back to their own. This process will reoccur until all of the participants have performed their object dance.
- In the next phase, as called by the facilitator, all of the participants are invited to begin to meet and interact with the other object dances at their own pace, even to the point of exchanging their objects, whenever and however they are moved to do so.
- In the next phase, again cued by the guide, the players are asked to dance their objects into the center of the space and create a composite sculpture with them, as they disengage and step back into a circle of observation.

A circle sharing at the end about the personal and collective experience is an essential closing act of the ritual.

Gary Gray engaged in an Object Dance at a Group Motion Retreat, 2008 (photograph courtesy Colin Harvey).

Variation

The Object Dance can be practiced with a particular focus on the chakras, the seven psychic-energy centers in the esoteric traditions of Hinduism and Tantric Buddhism. Each participant chooses one of the chakras that they feel drawn to, and moves with their object in connection to this energy center, exploring its particular physical, energetic, and emotional associations.

Reflection

Manfred—*The intuitive choice of object and or chakra is a vital element of the process. It initiates the ritual process of self-discovery and identification. The "extended body" of the Object Dancer creates a rich space of movement invention and image creation, with the potential of entering archetypal, surrealistic territories. The interactive aspect with both the object and other Object Dancers provides playful and unexpected emotional drama. For the observers, one could describe this dance as Performance Art.*

Group Activations

For 5–8 participants.
With live music.

- One of the participants sets up a group sculpture/tableaux, which may be physically connected or not, spatially clustered, or spread out.
- On a signal, the dancers in the group begin to move, motivated by both their individual, as well as group forms of expression and they bring it into life, playing out its inherent character, nature, kinesthetic potentiality.
- On another signal, the activator stops the dance when s/he feels it is complete, and brings it to stillness.
- S/he then will take the place of one of the dancers in the group, who will then become the next activator.
- The activator initiation can also have a verbal component—image, theme, idea, which will then feed into the activation.

Variation

- The verbal component may have the form of a poem, which will be read after the setting up is complete and just be listened to by the dancers.
- The dance will begin with a second reading, which can take creative liberty in its delivery, and extend through the whole poem.

Tableaux Stills

For 10 to 20 participants.
With or without live music.

- The group divides into movers and observers.
- On cue from a facilitator, "Lights off," the observers will close their eyes, and one of them will call out a theme, image or phrase.
- The movers will organize quickly into a tableaux realization of the theme.
- The facilitator will then signal, "Lights on," at which point the observers will open their eyes and observe the still tableaux.
- The facilitator signals, "Lights off," and the next image will be called.
- In the second round of play, the groups will switch roles.

- This form can be considered a composite between the style of the Self Portrait Dance and the Active-Passive solo form, expanded through the use of tableaux.

Reflection

Manfred—*This is a wonderful exercise in spontaneous group creation. It can be played with a sense of theatricality, or a sense of abstraction. The Tableaux Stills can be a composite of both.*

Group Tableaux Travel

For 6–8 participants, or more.
With live music.

- One of the participants sets up however many dancers s/he prefers in three separate tableaux, one after the other, requesting the dancers to remember each of the specific set ups.
- On a signal that may have verbal component—image, theme, idea, sentence—the activation dance will begin, "connecting the dots." It starts at the first of the three tableaux, and then travels to or through the second and third ones, informed by, and moving from the original shape, the thematic focus, and the interactive responses of the dancers, taking as much, or as little time as the collective body determines it needs.
- Passing through tableaux, one may or may not take a moment of stillness.
- The dance may end with the arrival at the third tableaux, or it may continue on, until the activator signals the ending, and the dance comes to stillness.
- Another activator will then choose his/her dancers and begin another round of Tableaux Travel.
- Live music is an important partner in the journey.

Variations

- In a performance setting, the engagement of the audience and the dancers can be heightened and intensified when audience members are invited to provide the themes, ideas, images, or phrases in written form, prior to the performance. Each activator/choreographer can choose from among these suggestions.

- A visual component can be added through live video projection of images, responding to the thematic focus, or the architecture of the dance and music, selected and drawn in the moment, from a video image bank.

Reflection

Manfred—*In all Activation Structures, a transmission of movement or sound from body to body, through touch or voice, from the activator to the dancer or group is the modus vivendi and creates the playful, creative interactivity propelled by both expectation and surprise. Each act of activation is a kind of birth giving, an organic evolution from the seed of a shape into the growing of a dance. There is a lot of joyful discovery at work: how the realization of the given form or idea might, or might not, meet the intention of the activator. Or how, on the other end, the receiver experiences the kind of form, or being they inspired the activator to shape them into, and where it takes them. It is also a great structure to facilitate movement invention, character formation, and the creation of instant choreography.*

Evolution Cycle

For groups from 5–20 participants.
With live music.
This score can serve both dancers and actors. It is a movement meditation on an evolutionary cycle from (a) plants to (b) animals to (c) humans to (d) humans gone insane back to (e) animals to (f) plants.

- Each participant has their own path of evolution, begun by their choice of plant, transforming into its respective animal being, transforming into the respective human character, and on the retrograde returning to their previous animal and plant form.
- This cycle will be realized on an individual basis, but can be interactive when desired.
- The change from one state to the other is fluid, but will be guided by the live music.
- The movement can range between abstract and theatrical, using sounds and words when desired.

Reflection

Manfred—*This structure is focused on becoming and being, rather than representing the particular evolutionary state. It wants to hone in on the essence of the particular form or character. Interactions are as random as possible, or not, as they are in the "real" world. On my visit to Ngorongoro, one of East Africa's most amazing animal reserves, I had an experience of witnessing a multitude of species roaming along the savannah. From there I went back to the "insanity" of civilized tourist life, wishing I was back with the animals.*

Past Lives Circle

For up to 20 participants.
With live music.

- The group of players is standing in a large circle with the eyes closed, and with space between each other, entering a meditative state. The focus of the meditation is "past lives," whatever that may mean to the participants.
- When ready, the first person moves inside the circle manifesting the past life form of theirs that has risen to their awareness, and spending as much time as they need, before going back into the circle.
- At any moment, another person who is ready enters, and another, and so on, co-existing and or interacting with the others' lives until returning to the circle.
- The past lives can be embodiments of any living thing that comes to mind, and can be danced, sounded, spoken in any "language" or form.
- The play goes on until ended by the silence of the facilitating music.
- A discussion after the dance will be fortuitous.

Reflection

Manfred—*The Past Lives Circle is a both meditative and playful ritual of investigating one's identity and heritage while exposing it to a circle of witnesses. What comes up is what matters, from a life form from ages* ago to one from yesterday, from a single cell to a famous historic being. There is no judgment of right or wrong, as memories can be accurate or vague, serious or silly.

Doing Nothing: The Dance of Stillness

For 5 to 50 participants.
With or without music.

- Stand or sit randomly in the space. This structure can be practiced in a studio or outdoors. It lends itself well to be practiced in a natural landscape.
- Remain in stillness, with a focus on inner sensations and listening, with your eyes open, yet without focus, gazing where your eyes have landed.
- Aim to come to a sense of centeredness, contacting others from this place of centeredness. As you move, observe yourself, noticing, testing areas of pain or comfort in your own body.
- Notice the slowing down of time. As your perception sharpens, you will observe more.
- This dance can unfold over time, 20 minutes to an hour, ending with a predetermined signal. Or it can remain open ended.

Reflection

Brigitta—*The Doing Nothing: Dance of Stillness structure was inspired by a workshop I took in New York City, in the late 1970s, with Daniel Lepkoff, one of the pioneers of Contact Improvisation.*

It offers time for self-exploration and self-observation. In this place of stillness, we notice where we are in our body, observe our posture, our thoughts, and become aware of the space and people around us. We notice how we are, and where we want to be in this very moment, at this particular time and space, and with the people in this space. There is no demand, no expectation to make something happen, no need to please or follow social norms. Gradually, we will notice that our perception changes. Becoming aware of "where we want to be," we follow those inner prompts when they come into our consciousness. This may indicate a change of posture, a walk, crawl, or traveling of sorts to a different place, joining another person in the space, making contact, or moving away. In this contacting and moving away, we include the environment—walls, trees, water, whatever may be available in a given setting.

Our lives are filled with lots of noise. The vibration of voices, cars, music of various kinds enters into our ears and resonates into our bodies. When we think of dance, we mostly consider that music will be there and is part of the source. If I have music—the music gives me clues. It triggers my bones, my muscles, my nerves, where and how I feel. In dance, feeling is like an organ that I rely on—I feed on—it is tied in with my breathing. It also connects me with the person across the room. I can feel when it connects—when it clicks in. As our perceptions change, there is a sense of hearing each other and our selves in stillness. In this practice, there is a sense of nothingness—stillness—timelessness—a sense of being at the right time at the right place. It is a place of no thinking, only being. No thing.

Game Sequences

Dance Games can also be played in predetermined sequences. The advantage of Game Sequences is that the dancers can experience a longer improvisation, as the change of structure renews their energy. The sequence also gives an overall dynamic to the improvisation. Music plays a very important part in cuing the beginning, the end, and in offering transitions.

The examples given here are just a few of the suggestions that can be made. Other combinations are of course possible, as long as they allow organic transitions between the different parts.

Example I
A. The dancers begin with the Area Game, in three areas, accompanied by music.
B. The music stops and the action stops.
C. The dancers in the three areas evolve into three groups and a Trialogue Game begins, without music.
D. The three groups gradually come together to form one large group. The music begins again.
E. The sequence ends.

Example II
A. The dancers begin the Mirror Game, accompanied by music.
B. The Active-Passive Game evolves as one person in each mirror pair closes his eyes, becoming passive.

C. All the passive dancers are eventually connected into one group. All of the active dancers become passive and part of this passive group.
D. When the whole group is connected, one dancer in the center will begin the first Crystallization impulse. The Crystallization Game then follows.
E. The sequence ends as the music stops.

Example III

A. The sequence begins with an Adding Game, without music.
B. A Time Dance Game is begun as one person breaks away from the adding circle to initiate a basic movement. The music begins at this time.
C. One dancer freezes and begins a Crystallization Game.
D. The Crystallization ends when one dancer forms the crystal, but does not give an impulse. The music stops.
E. The central dancer energizes the group with his/her voice, as each dancer responds according to the Receiving Energy Game.
F. The sequence ends.

Introduction to the Friday Night Workshop

The Workshop arose in 1971 from a Group Motion dance studio practice session, led by the verbal guidance from Brigitta in interaction with live music created by Manfred and other musicians. A specific series of guided movement meditations focused on breath, sound, and movement qualities was channeled by Brigitta and emerged as the blueprint for the Friday Night Workshop. As a practice of structures and interactive games of movement expression, communication, and play, it evolved. Now a ritual facilitated by Brigitta's voice and percussion, or Manfred and his voice and keyboard, it has its own life in the hands of their students. The Workshop was informed by Brigitta's studies in awareness practices and holistic healing, human energy, and dance/movement therapy. Her masters in somatic psychology, along with Manfred's years of practice with the Group Motion Workshop and professional company, and his teaching of dance improvisation at the University of the Arts, all have shaped what the workshop offers. During the decades, the workshop has kept its basic original concept and structure intact.

Manfred Fischbeck and Brigitta Herrmann leading a Friday Night Workshop, 2015 (photograph courtesy Bill Hebert).

Model of Group Motion on a Friday Night

For 6 to 100 participants.

This format follows a very specific sequence, throughout a two-hour session.

With music.

1. Gathering and Preparation

    Entering the space: the participants and musicians gather, orient themselves, greet each other, and settle into the space. The musicians, in numbers between one and ten, unpack and tune their instruments as the participants find a place on the floor.

2. Guided Meditation

    Lying on their backs, the participants relax, get grounded, and focus on breathing during a guided meditation. The facilitator guides their breathing into specific parts of the body, beginning at the feet and moving towards the head. Through this guided meditation, with minimal musical accompaniment, an increased

Manfred and Brigitta, near the windows, guide the Beginning Meditation, Friday Night Workshop, 2015 (photograph courtesy Bill Hebert).

awareness and ambiance is created. A sense of body/mind union can be experienced.

3. Warm Up

    Following the meditation, a transition leads from conscious breathing into stretching. The stretching dance involves the entire body, including the face. It progresses gradually to move towards an upright position, onto the feet. Each person's timing, focus, and expression evolves and changes from one moment to the next. You will see that no two people move in the same way. All instructions are based on instantaneous decisions and depend on the energy of the group, yet follow a specific sequence. The sequence may vary in length, in terms used, and in their explicitness.

4. Isolation

    Instructions focus on originating movement from various parts of the body.

    "Move from your feet. Let the feet lead, initiating movement from your feet."

    Participants enter into forms of dialogue and are invited to alternate moving on their own or explore playing with others.

Participants perform the Traveling Dance, Friday Night Workshop, 2015 (photograph courtesy Bill Hebert).

5. States of Being and Textures

    This section suggests themes, structures, or images. Some suggestions are: "Connected to Strings," "Transparency," "Balance," "Off-Balance," "Moving Like an Animal of Your Choice," "Choose a Color and Find the Dance of this Color," "Move From the Shape or Form You Find Yourself In," "Add a State of Being: Nervousness, Loneliness, Frustration, Determination, Forcefulness, Clarity," etc. Increased awareness of space and expression are elements of this section.

6. Structures of Relationship

    Instructions call to mirror or dialogue with others. Eye contact may be initiated.

7. Shadow Dance

    Participants are instructed to move, following one person in a line formation, or in an organized spatial formation. In this way, small or large groups evolve into fantastic, often mythical, choreographic landscapes. Leading and following each other changes according to the initiative of each move—moving slow, fast, or ecstatically at one time, with something similar or different at another. Patterns of spirals, circles, or circular clusters often include sounds and voices from participants. A sense of ritual space and of community is created during this section.

8. Active Passive Dance

In finalizing the two-hour session, this dance is about touch and trust. In partnership, one of the participants is instructed to close his/her eyes, allowing the other to guide, sculpt, and move him/her. After a certain amount of time, participants are instructed to switch roles. The sense of integration, play, and communication is subtle, intimate, and caring.

9. Closing

Participants, facilitators, and musicians sit together, forming a circle, and are encouraged to share about their experiences with the dance and music. During this closing circle, articulating, sharing, and rerouting the nonverbal experience into verbal expression may reveal surprising insights.

10. The Role of Music

The music spans from synthesizer to drums, and traditionally includes wind instruments and voice. All music is created spontaneously during the session and is an equal and essential component of the Friday Night Workshop. The infinite variety of offerings by the various musicians resonates with the dance in a constant flow of dynamic changes. It aids and stimulates play and communications amongst the participants. The breath of the music and dance are woven together, creating a unified whole. The live music mirrors the energy of the dance—moment to moment—and provides an environment of stimulation and support throughout.

Reflections

Brigitta—*These game forms guide participants into spontaneous exchange and heightened awareness that create dreamlike landscapes, and evoke archetypal images. As a sacred space for communication that is deep and direct, it has touched the lives of thousands of people in many parts of the word—Germany, France, Argentina, Barbados and Japan. The dynamic interplay between the improvised music and dance serve as a mirror for each other. Group Motion Workshops allow for meditative and* ecstatic play, for physical and spiritual presence. It is guiding participants into a place of authenticity with self and others, for personal and collective journeys, and can serve as an agent for healing.

* * *

Manfred—*Everybody has the ability to dance, to move, to express themselves with their body. The structure of the Friday Night Workshop is designed in a way that anyone can move in it and find his/her own dance. But the space is always shared with others; everyone affects and learns from each other. The live music is the field of energy that connects everyone. The Group Motion Workshop celebrates the language of movement as a*

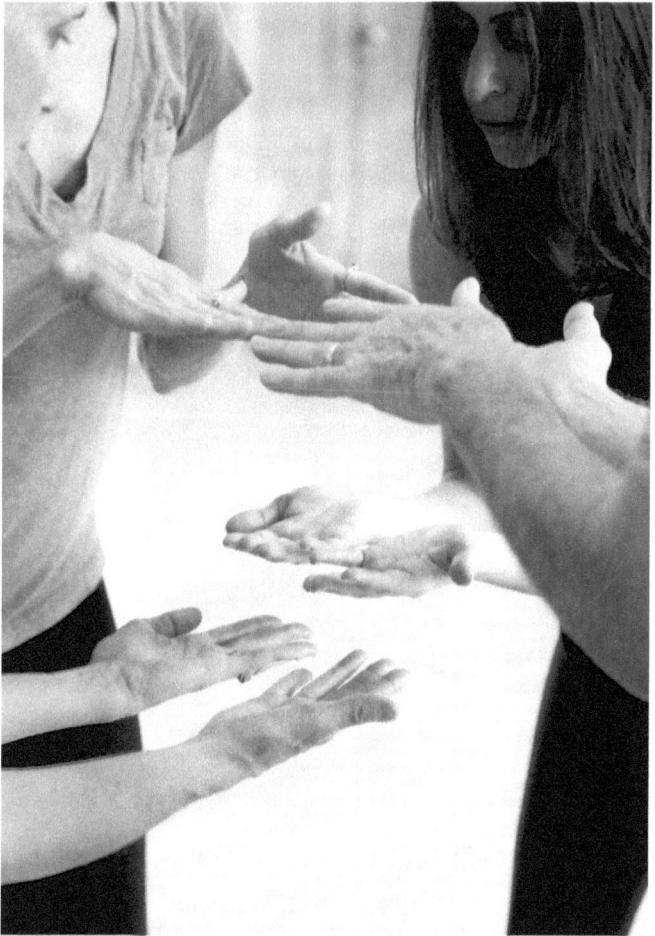

Hand Dance, Friday Night Workshop, 2015 (photograph courtesy Bill Hebert).

language that anyone can speak and understand. It creates a ritual space for building and celebrating community.

The Friday Night Workshop incorporates larger numbers of movers and energies, yet the guiding principle is one of surrender to the guided interactive structure, to the larger picture of the common good for all. To accept different roles such as leading and following, talking and listening, being active or passive will grow the sense of community, not as a limitation, but as an expanding and freeing force for each individual. The listening to the authentic impulse within oneself, and the others, will result in connections and initiatives and creative visions of the whole that is larger than the sum of its parts, generating at times instant choreographic images or landscapes that no one person could possibly imagine.

* * *

Participants wrote:

> This form of expression is an alternative form of communication far deeper than words, and more real and more honest than normal interaction. The workshop has changed my life.

* * *

Contact Dance with Renee Kurz (*left*), Gary Gray and Nina Sherak, Friday Night Workshop, 2015 (photograph courtesy Bill Hebert).

Delicious.

* * *

It replenishes me.

* * *

It helps me escape from my head, come out of my shell.

* * *

People say, how can you do the same thing night after night? But it is always different. Just take stretching ... each time I find a new way, and sometimes I'll see someone stretching in yet another way, and I will be inspired to do that.

* * *

I deeply feel that the risk, the trust, the joy, and the adventure are vital ways of reclaiming the power of sacred dance.

* * *

Group Motion creates opportunities for me to gain insight about my own life and my relationship with others. The structures serve as metaphors for life and relationships. As I fully engage in the structures, my body leads me to discoveries in all areas of my life.

* * *

Djuna Wojton, Spiritual Healer:

Group Motion creates a safe space in an alcohol/drug free environment that enables you to connect with others on a deep authentic level that inspires well-being, community and personal groups.

In the workshops, I learned to be able to quiet the chattering of my mind and listen to my body's intelligence. I learned to walk backwards in a room of full of other people also walking backwards, and didn't collide with anyone. I also learned how to "do nothing." A great process to clear away the clutter in my mind and open the door to true creativity which enabled me to sizzle on the floor like a slice of bacon frying in a skillet, soar through the sky with a flock of birds, and howl at the moon with a pack of wolves. I have been rocked like a baby, was literally swept off my feet and carried away across the room, and twirled round and round by my partner, much like the games I enjoyed on the playground as a child.

* * *

Gary Gray, Participant:

I came to my first Group Motion Friday Night Workshop in 1992; I was in my mid-forties. My relationship to dance up to then was complicated by my childlike impulse to move with freedom, joy, and connection, and my adolescent/adult aversion to exposure, ridicule, and shame, which comes from not being a "good" dancer. I was caught between wanting to dance and not wanting to feel bad about not being good at it. I don't remember how long it took for me to become really addicted to Group Motion, but I do remember the relief and expansiveness that came from experiencing that Group Motion was not about doing it right; it was about doing it wholeheartedly.

Now it is 25 years later, and I am in my early seventies and still attending at least

40 Group Motion workshops each year. Along the way, I have attended Group Motion retreats in Bermuda, Barbados, Colorado, Arizona, Massachusetts, and West Virginia. I have danced with a few who are no longer living, and I have danced with a few who were not yet born when I found Group Motion. Along the way, it has become my favorite fitness workout and, more surprisingly, my favorite spiritual practice. For me, spirituality is the process of becoming a whole self in relationship with others and the environment. The Group Motion process invites me first to come into awareness and relationship to the movement of my body, beginning with breath, and moving on to stretching, crawling, and finally, connecting with others. This slow awakening invites intimacy with my own body, before I am invited into intimate connection with others. It allows me to experience what Martin Buber called "I–Thou" relationships, another name for spirituality.

* * *

Melanie Rios Glaser, Movement Artist:

Friday nights led by Manfred and Brigitta for dancers and non-dancers alike was a terrific communal experience. As improvisation can be intimidating to beginners, following simple suggestions of what to invent next came easily. Instructions led to engaging other people in innovative ways that created rapport. Those evenings are a testament of the power of dance to bring people together, to celebrate community and to explore the joy of dancing. As the evening came to a close, there was a unified and satisfying sigh, after the rich experience. Benevolence was in the mind of all participants.

* * *

Sarah Manno, Dance Teacher:

Since Brigitta, Hellmut and I were students together during my year at the Mary Wigman Studio in West Berlin, I have admired their work and enjoyed their friendship. After they formed Group Motion with Manfred and eventually moved the company to the USA, we resumed contact. I have over the years attended their performances and participated in workshops, which have nourished my Wigman roots and enriched my own teaching of dance. These days improvisation is markedly lacking in many modern or contemporary dance classes as focus on technique has taken over. What a loss. There is room and need for both. Improvisation is a time for spontaneous movement that emanates from within or is a response to another's moves and Group Motion's Movement Games create a way to make this comfortable for students at all levels. Never do I teach a modern class without including one of about half a dozen of these games gleaned from their work. As soon as students realize they are having a spontaneous, nonverbal conversation, inhibitions fade.

* * *

Silvana Cardell, Dancer, Choreographer:

The Group Motion Improvisation workshop is at the core of my professional dance training. I truly value the inclusion of both trained and amateur dancers. This participation allows resourceful collective and individual interpretations of the given improvisation scores. Whether to reach states of self-awareness or to develop my own choreographic structures, Manfred Fischbeck and Brigitta Herrmann have influenced my work and enriched my life.

* * *

Rita Feliciano, Dance Critic for the *San Francisco Bay Guardian*, contributor to *Dance View Magazine* and *Dance View Times*:

> Perhaps Group Motion's most wide-ranging contribution to Philadelphia is its Friday Night Workshop. What struck the outside observer was the freedom with which these participants—a social worker, a teacher, a psychologist, an entrepreneur and scientist, among others—interacted with each other. Their vulnerability and their acceptance of each other was extraordinary. However temporary, however utopian, they had created a community of like-minded people. Most remarkable was the sheer beauty of some of these so spontaneously found improvisations. Mary Wigman would have understood and celebrated this legacy.

The Significance of Ritual Dances

Brigitta and Manfred—We know of indigenous cultural practices involving dance in a tribal relationship, honoring birth, fertility, and initiation. Some of these forms have been reinstated, taken from African or Native American cultures in an attempt to reconnect to the past, or as a

Closing Circle lead by Manfred and Brigitta, Friday Night Workshop, 2015 (photograph courtesy Bill Hebert).

way to acknowledge the losses of the past. Seen and practiced in dance programs at colleges or dance schools, and offered as part of a repertoire of steps and combinations, they seemed frequently detached from their authentic origin. In addition, since the development of the industrial age, in Western cultures, we have seen a decline of integration with the intuitive arts, and with nature. While some forms of expression through dance occur in discos and dance halls, they are usually geared towards sexual innuendo. Very few alternative venues are offered for a community, involving a form of ritual, inclusive of creative dance, music, and play.

And now, the contemporary ritual is based in social media, with even less physical contact. Instead we use phones and computers and through television, our emotional constructs based on consumption and competition. How much time do we and our children spend in front of screens? Our creative energy is primarily channeled into intellectual processes which assume specific norms, norms of interest, understanding, and ability. The individual's uniqueness and his/her needs are in question, streamlined and compromised. There is little room for ritual that supports holistic and authentic sharing. The constraint of creative self-expression results in disease, depression, eating disorders, antisocial behaviors, and addictions. On a daily basis we are informed and conditioned with stories documenting the misuse of drugs and health problems related to obesity.

There is a movement ritual in the Group Motion repertory that does have a striking analog in "real" life; the Impulse Circle is a miniature form of The Wave done in sports stadiums. Both, the group ritual and the crowd wave are a form rooted in biology, physics and ecology. We have waves, chain reactions, and domino effects. We speak of waves "going viral," and witness a small gesture gathering speed and mass. Honeybees wave en masse to signal threats, concert goers and sports enthusiasts do a wave out of pure joy. Both can be seen as dance. One can say that most all structures and games in the Group Motion practice are rituals of varying sizes.

In Activation, an activator shapes the passive partner or group into a desired form and expression. On signal, this form then comes into motion, and they dance the given form until stopped by another signal and are re-directed, re-shaped into another. This structure can be seen as a ritual of animation. The Village Dance actually combines individual and group, private and public, rituals in overlapping or simultaneous and ever changing ways. If we can imagine a village with glass houses situated around a square, where all of the actions and activities are transparent and visible to all at all times, where people have the choice of being at home or visiting other homes, or staying in the public square at any given moment—we might have a utopian life of mutual co-existence and tolerance. We find that in the arena of dance and play, this utopia is possible and provides a degree of freedom and empowerment we can otherwise only dream of. One can call this an altered state that is at all times aware and concerned with the common good. It is driven by an inherent spirituality of spontaneous expression and communication, of resonance and empathy with the whole.

In a more structural and detailed analysis, the Village Dance can and is likely to combine, utilize and process, inside or outside the houses, a variety of other structures such as the Mirror Game, the Time Dance Game, the Message Game, the Grid, the Crystallization Game, and other sound and touch and verbalization structures. All of these structures and games have rules that are there, not to win or overpower each other, but to communicate and co-create, and they can be broken in the process of co-creating.

Participants explore the Activation Dance, Group Motion Retreat at Crestone Mountain Zen Center, Colorado, 2008 (photograph courtesy Colin Harvey).

When performed in a performance setting, it is important that the audience knows the rules and can follow the unfolding of the dance, the choice making, the different applications of sub-structures, the breaking of the rules. It will have a richer experience, similarly to listening to the performance of a fugue in music, with the knowledge of the fugue structures, or following the ritual of a sports game by being familiar with the rules. It is the transporting power of ritual in any form or circumstance, that the players and observers share this knowledge in the experience of the spontaneous realization and celebration of it. Another large ritual structure, the Group Tableaux Travel Dance, often based on a theme suggested by the audience, involves an activator setting up three different group tableaux in different spatial formations, and then activates them to travel from one to the other, to the other. The individual and collective choice making of the dancers during this traveling provides insight into the creative process of ritualized group creativity.

When practiced in the outdoors, as Group Motion has done on many occasions, live music might imitate nature sounds, and even incorporate found objects and materials such as rocks and branches with the voicing. We have danced on the beaches, in botanic gardens, and in a desert mountain terrain, echoing sounds of the birds, winds, and moving water.

Doing Nothing, The Dance of Stillness, (*left to right*) Nina Sherak, Katy Bank, Sophia Trovato and Gary Gray. Friday Night Workshop, 2015 (photograph courtesy Bill Hebert).

The Group Motion Company has been very invested and explorative in the drive to create site specific performances. Indoor or outdoor interactive dances within a chosen site in public spaces by their nature have a ritual aspect to them, as they illuminate and relate to the site in a non-conventional way. They engage the audience in active participation such as following the travel of the dance or the play. Dancers of Group Motion danced as a sizable audience was following them down the Benjamin Franklin Parkway of Philadelphia. The site specific tour traveled along the sites of notable public art such as the Holocaust sculpture, the Love Sculpture, the Rodin Museum's Gate of Hell, and his Thinker, creating ritual dances paying homage and interacting with sculpture in a dialogic way. A well-known Philadelphia choral conductor commented that he had never seen these art works in this way before.

The ritual nature of site specific performances, especially those that are improvised, also creates a deeper connection between the dancers/movers and their audiences. By sharing the in-the-moment creation performed in an every day life setting, incidental passers-by get pulled into the experience, even if they are resistant or bewildered at first. And yet they stay on and watch intently and with apparent engagement.

The largest and most encompassing Rituals of Group Motion are the workshop retreats. Lasting for the duration of a week-end or a whole week,

Climbing the dunes in a Group Motion Retreat at the Great Sand Dunes National Park, Colorado, 2008 (photograph courtesy Colin Harvey).

Two women from the Group Motion Retreat at the Great Sand Dunes National Park, Colorado, 2008 (photograph courtesy Colin Harvey).

the retreats take place in special locations in special natural environments. These locations have included dance centers on the coast of Maine, the Islands of Bermuda and Barbados, and Sarasota, Florida; the Urban Laboratory of Arcosanti, Arizona, the Crestone Mountain Zen Center in Colorado, The Claymont Seminar Retreat Center in West Virginia and the Earth Dance Center in Fairfield, Massachusetts. Two daily two-to-three hour sessions, one in the morning and one in the evening are offered. The mornings explore and practice the Group Motion structures and games in a specially selected sequence; the evenings celebrate the Friday Night Workshop format in different variations. Excursions into nature provide additional site specific dance experience, offering an expanded opportunity for creative growth, healing and transformation.

One can argue that our globalizing multi-cultural, diverse, and segregated modern mass society is in dire need for new rituals of art for all people, that go beyond competitive winning or losing and transcend nationalist, racist or religious exclusivity in order to serve the larger space of global compassion. The Group Motion Workshop Rituals were created from this need.

* * *

Participants wrote:

In a time of this global culture, where there is so much divisiveness, conflict, trauma, uncertainty, Group Motion has held many of us in its arms. We can then

Dancers reclining on sand during a Group Motion Retreat at the Great Sand Dunes National Park, Colorado, 2008 (photograph courtesy Colin Harvey).

go out into the wide world and hold others in our own way. This is to me, the miracle of Group Motion. The structures Group Motion provides are ones that are relationship enhancing. The Mirror, the Dialogue, the meditation, the trust required in the Active-Passive, the Shadow Dance, the Triangle, The Grid, are all relationally enhancing structures. The moving through space on your own, the shape and form that you find yourself in, the dance of colors, transparency, glass, slow motion, moving like someone you know, make a person more familiar with themselves, more comfortable in their own skin. This enhances the self and the self in relationship.

* * *

And what about art, music, dance, as key elements of the Group Motion culture? I feel grateful that there is a place where my creativity is not only appreciated, but is as essential as breathing. I yearn for a culture in the larger world where this is true. I am deeply grateful for Group Motion, and that I am part of a community in which there is active sacredness going on.

* * *

Group Motion brings people together and gives them an exercise where they can communicate with each other in unconventional ways ... with movement symbols instead of linguistic signals. If I am right, it could help explain why people have a hard time describing Group Motion workshop experiences. The experience, being nonverbal is therefore hard to talk about.. . It is more like a dream than a waking experience. Perhaps because, like in dreams, it can be hard to even remember what

Top: Participants engage with nature at a Group Motion Retreat in Sarasota, Florida, 2007 (photograph courtesy Group Motion). *Bottom:* Descending a dune, Group Motion Retreat at the Great Sand Dunes National Park, Colorado, 2008 (photograph courtesy Colin Harvey).

Indoor play by participants in a Group Motion Retreat at Arcosanti, Arizona, 2013 (photograph courtesy Group Motion).

happened, much less express these experiences in words, they seem more mysterious, perhaps even mystical. I felt often like I am in a trancelike state, and I assume others feel similarly.

* * *

Words, we know, can lie. We are practiced in telling stories in ways that might not tell all the truth, or might hide some of the truth, or might be completely fake. At Group Motion, it seems to me, the thought of lying, of trying to hide who you are, or what you are feeling—well it just doesn't come up. Who would want to lie? What possible motive could you have for doing so?

* * *

The closing ritual of the workshop is the circle at the end, where people have a chance to identify themselves and say something about their experience that evening. It is a transition back from the world of no words into the ordinary world where we talk in order to communicate. It's a way of trying to remember that which is hard to remember because it happened without words. It's a way of sharing individual experiences so others can learn what it was like, from another perspective. Sometimes, maybe even once every few months, someone will say they wish that this world leader, or that world leader would come to the workshop. Usually these are world leaders who are in conflict at the moment. Everyone nods knowingly when the person makes this comment.

* * *

The Group Motion workshop can make you feel like good things are possible. Like understanding is possible. Like resolution—a healing, peaceful, cooperative resolution—is possible. Group Motion provides a sense of completion. People can express who they are.

* * *

While each workshop uses and creates ritual, no single workshop is the same as any other. In fact, the dance changes so much, it may at times, seem like chaos. The way order almost always arises out of this chaos seems magical. The workshop promotes a safe, healing space for expression, allowing dancers to lower the self-protective masks that usually buffer their relations with others. The movement structures enable people to invent and understand a language of movement that allows them to express their authentic selves. This invented movement language helps participants go far beyond the expectations that we have of common dance interactions, to create something much more valuable than just having a good time. It is something that feels like it can make an enormous, positive difference in the world.

* * *

My definition of dance has become much bigger, broader, and richer. Group Motion is a place to reconnect with my body, tap into its grounding and wisdom, and see what emerges... an exquisite dance of trust, caring, tenderness, or an emotive dance of anger, confusion or play.

* * *

I have observed, and experienced the healing power of the dance.... Group Motion has simply become the place where I feel that I am the most completely me.

Part II.
Group Motion Practices

Eight Therapeutic Principles of Group Motion

The following eight therapeutic principles are essential to our practice: altered states of consciousness, intuition, breathing, transformation, ritual, play, balance, and communication.

1. Altered States of Consciousness

    The creative process has something to do with shifting consciousness. The shaman communicates with the spirit world in a state of altered consciousness, or what Carlos Castaneda (1975) has called "non-ordinary" reality.

    We can work from weakness to strength, from pain to pleasure, from isolation to wholeness. It demands from the one who seeks healing to move beyond the comfort zone of the habitual, and face the shadow to be able to tell the truth. We all are familiar with the phrase, "the truth will set you free." It has been said that telling the truth re-generates the energy that was made stuck by the lie, both in ourselves and in the people with whom we share it. Energy is released and regenerated as we align with our essential selves. It also urges us to enter unknown places, to go beyond the personal. We may call it the perception of the heart when we shift from ego to wholeness. In this sense, the perception of who we are is the doorway into being versus becoming, and dance and movement can facilitate embodiment, being present in the body at a given moment. The aspect of gaining present moment awareness is itself the focus of many spiritual traditions. By discovering our own authentic dance, we can find our place within the layers of the universal dance. We experience an altered state of consciousness, a shifted perspective, when our conscious and subconscious minds communicate with each other.

2. Intuition

    In the Group Motion context, intuition is emphasized as a guide for stimulating self-expression, playful interaction, and creativity among the participants. As one participant said, "A Group Motion workshop becomes the container for the integrity of the higher self, the authentic self and the intuitive self to come through." The deeper dimensions are honored and expressed, like dreaming. Just as we know that we can fly, move, feel, smell and dance in our dreams, we have access to deeper dimensions when the dream consciousness is acted upon through movement. Through practice, participants movements and inner processes become more familiar and they are able to tap into deeper dimensions of an intuitive reality.

3. Breathing

"Breathing is the bridge between two worlds. It spans the borderline between control and no control, between the taught and the untaught." (Keleman, 1981, P. 134). When a child is born and takes its first breath, she is separating from the body of the mother and connecting full to her own. A new life and consciousness has begun. With this first breath, a movement passes through the body of the child, an incredible sensation of life, the first dance of breath, sound, and movement together. In dance, we are aiming for this togetherness.

This breath functions like a barometer. It indicates the pressure of the atmosphere of each moment, disclosing the mood of a person. Or, one may think of it as a seismograph, measuring the earth's vibrations. The breath reveals an infinite scale of nuances. Every amount of pressure and release, or holding of rhythmic or melodic articulation can be observed. It may be visible to the eye, or felt by a sense of empathy and compassion. We can know how someone feels by mirroring his/her breath.

In the therapeutic context, breath becomes a tool for self-regulation for the therapist and the client, as there is the understanding that the direct access to emotions is through the body, and the primary pathway to the body is the breath. In the context of the Group Motion experience, the dancing participants may override their habitual fears or threats through playing with their breath, trying new ways of breathing, breathing deeper and connecting with themselves. These exercises can be used to encourage participants experiment with synchronicity of movement and breath, and to trace the impact of this connection.

4. Transformation

How do we know when something is transformed? In the context of performances, whether in dance, music, or theater, transformation is the practice and the aim. The same is true in the therapeutic context. Unique to both is the process of truth-searching, and the understanding of letting vulnerability become visible and conscious. In the context of dance, the movement itself may lead to a new place, particularly under the guidance of the coach or choreographer. The body itself is the medium of transformation and becomes very concrete during the creative process. In this way, the human being is in a constant work in progress. We allow ourselves to become acquainted with the fact of change as an element of life. As we turn into water, fire, air, or take on the quality of a character, we become this element or character, practicing the transformation, guided by our imagination.

5. Ritual

> "The root for ritual means 'to fit together.' Through drama and song, cadence and dance, and various other components, shamans ritually fit together pieces of energy that become the essence and pattern of life. Without these pieces, the earth cannot move, the tribe cannot continue, and magic ceases.—Telesco, 2000, p. 3

Ritual is a container. The dance that manifests in ritual gives external expression to psychic realities and includes elements of play and spontaneity. Ritual offers familiarity through its repeatable values, and therefore it also offers a sense of safety. Monica Steiner underlines this by saying: "Rituals help to alleviate anxiety. They provide a framework, in which a frightened person holds on to the familiar in order to contain difficult thoughts and feelings" (Payne, 1992, p. 149). Ritual is a helpful and valuable container for working with groups or individuals. The set up, the space, the order of events, all provide a sense of home and grounding. Dance ritual also links us to the beginning of civilization as a bridge between self and the cosmos.

All over the world, people of all cultures, past and present, create rituals in support of values, order, and in celebration of life's events. "The existence and prosperity of a ... tribe are absolutely bound up with the scrupulous and traditional performance of the ceremonies," wrote Jung. (1966, P. 97). Ritual is known as a form that bridges the realities between consciousness and unconsciousness. It is a space where emotion can turn into motion. The most important events in our lives such as birth, marriage, and death were embedded in ritual and still are to a certain extent. Yet, in Western medicine, healing rituals consist of precarious procedures and divisions. Each specialization engages in a specific modality from surgery to drug therapy to psychotherapy. These rituals consist of filling out forms, having your temperature measured, your blood pressure taken, ultra sound, mammogram, or other sophisticated electronically manipulated tests. There is a lack of wholeness in most of these procedures.

"Ritual acts like a blueprint for the spiritual energy that you want to draw into your reality. Each time you work with a given design it becomes easier to create the associated energy." (Telesco, 2000, p. 42). Within this ritual structure of Group Motion, the group energy can be seen evolving to ecstatic heights, to a mystical union among the participants.

One participant wrote:

> For me, the heart of Group Motion is that it is always new. In some ways, this is a paradox, because I just said Group Motion has a ritualistic nature. However, at Group Motion, the ritual is in reinventing ritual, not in recreating the specific form of a particular ritual. At Group Motion, the rituals are constantly renewing themselves in order to meet the needs of the participants.

6. Play

Observing children at play, we are enchanted by their purity and grace. A child, deeply engaged in play does not reflect upon her doing. She doesn't think, "How do I look? Am I doing it right? Am I playing beautifully?" In the same moment that these kinds of thoughts emerge, the play stops. Artists and scientists have written about how discoveries were made during playing or dreaming. Mary Wigman's teacher, Rudolf Laban writes:

> In young animals and children we call it play, and in adults we call it acting and dancing. During play, efforts are tried out, selected and chosen as those best suited. The best effort becomes selected and habitual. (1950, p. 21).

The innate curiosity and desire for human interactions finds satisfaction by the element of play, and recovers an open-minded space. Both in play and dream-like states, the consciousness sinks into the body; time is forgotten. Echoing Freud, Nachmanovitch writes:

> Without play, learning and evolution are impossible. Play is the taproot from which original art springs; it is the raw stuff that the artist channels and organizes with all his learning and technique" (1990, p 42).

In our culture, one that largely opposes creativity and non-competitive play, the creative element of play is driven out of us early in life. We know of parents' remarks such as, "You can't play here." "There is not time to play." Or "Go and play," which is similar to "Leave me alone." In school, play becomes almost dangerous. So we associate play and its particular state of consciousness with guilt, blame, fear, shame, and disgrace. Despite all of the negative connotations, the state of mind during play reveals undisturbed beauty, fostering renewal and re-creation. During play, an act of self-creation, healing is imminent, an opportunity for authentic self-expression and communication without conscious effort.

7. Balance

We know that the earth's magnetism draws certain forces. Our own bodies, linked to this magnetism, do the same. We too are connected to the principles of negative-positive, feminine-masculine, or as in Chinese culture, yin-yang. As a principle life force by which our life is experienced, the polarity asks for a continuous balancing of those forces.

As a tree grows, it divides into two opposing principles. The first refers to the movement down with its roots, deep into the ground, into the earth. It is following the earth's magnetism, its gravitational force. At the same time, it moves upward, above the earth's crust toward the light, defying the force of gravity. We too are bound to this physical world and we balance ourselves between the two forces. Throughout our lives, we choose subconsciously or unconsciously between those principles, as well as the principles of contraction and expansion. The Group Motion experience of dance and music supports the achievement of balance. We recognize the balance that lies within each of us, and we must take responsibility for it, our own balance, harmony, and well-being as part of the whole.

When we dance from a soul level, from an intuitive place, sexual differences are not as evident as the energetic differences. It is independent of gender, so that any interactive combination can be experienced. When dancing from a soul level, we naturally move towards pleasure, towards energy increase, towards wholeness, towards balance. If we are out of balance, we can express this by moving with it and dancing it. Maybe we will tumble or fall, collapse or stumble, embodying and being truthful to our state of being at that moment. In doing so, we re-establish balance. When our energy flows freely, we come back to our own uniqueness, and feel once again in balance.

We may feel drawn to certain elements more than to others: water, fire, earth, air, or mountains, oceans, deserts. We may search for these with our imagination. We could imagine ourselves to be like a mandala, a devise for balance, bringing the elements and images in relationship to one another. The Group Motion dance movement ritual is itself reminiscent of a living, moving mandala. We can invite and allow the missing elements to be received. In homeopathy, acupuncture, or shiatsu treatments, energy is balanced to restore healing. If unobstructed and listened to, our innate sense for healing gears us towards wholeness, as innate as breath.

In Group Motion we practice giving and receiving and explore our preferences. We adhere to the degree of energy that is familiar to us by attracting or pushing away, expanding or contracting ourselves.

8. Communication

Through dancing, we enter into relationships with others. There is opportunity for playful dialogue, for mirroring, giving and receiving. When dancing, we do not have to engage in social formality to engage in intimacy. In the context of the ritual setting, you have the permission to communicate directly, in unconditional ways, without detour. The elements of kinesthetic sensation and the play of it allow for greater intensity. The relationship happens now, in the present moment of play, and in the joy of it. In Group Motion dance, we can choose our place, our expression, our distance or closeness, without consideration of decorum. We learn with each other, while discovering ourselves.

There are numerous techniques of touch with numerous variations in the context of dance: Contact Improvisation, lifting and holding techniques in ballet, holding and guiding in folk and social dances. Other arenas of touch come from massage and hands-on healing: Therapeutic Touch, Reiki, Feldenkreis, and Alexander Technique. We know touch can heal and it can also harm. The extent to which we feel comfortable touching others and being touched, as in our boundaries of touch, are all part of a learned pattern determined by cultural and social norms. Those norms are often religious and gender based, and do not necessarily correspond with an individual's needs for boundaries.

Group Motion is a forum where nurturing touch can be experienced and relearned, where boundaries can be practiced and re-negotiated and playfully incorporated. The permission to touch offers trust and reorientation, amplifying its physical, spiritual, and emotional dimensions. In the Group Motion Workshop, touch is integrated into the dance. The observer may see a subtle touch where people dialogue with each other by touching hands to extend a nurturing massage-like touch, or a sculpting of the body during an Active-Passive Game. It is a form that requires trust between the active/guiding person while the passive one has her eyes closed. It is a challenging, relationship enhancing form of play, well liked by both children and adults. Comments often address the issue of trust, and of an unexpected challenge or comfort in either of the roles, active or passive.

The Partnership of Dance and Music

Manfred—The dance-live music relationship in the improvisational work of Group Motion holds a space of uniqueness and essentialness, both in the workshop/class and the performance context. The connection between dance and music is celebrated as a sacred union from the beginning of human culture. From the initial moment of creation in the Friday Night Workshop—to thousands of subsequent Friday Nights—to hundreds of retreats and performances of the Company, at home and on tour—this symbiosis of dance and live music interaction is a vital and integral aspect of Group Motion's life.

Many of the structures and games of Group Motion are working in interactive partnership with live improvised music. The exceptions are structures that apply live sound, generated by the dance/movement itself, vocally or physically—clapping, stamping, brushing, or through the use of sounding objects—or silence. In the interactive play of dance and live music, sometimes one of the two has the lead while the other follows. At other times, both are playing with equal, simultaneous initiation. They may be moving in parallel, or in unison, or they may be in counter point, or contrast with each other. But at all times, this interactivity is one of partnership and dialogue, not one of being subservient to, or merely accompanying the other.

* * *

Brigitta—Dance and music become a unified whole in support of ritual and play. I often surprise myself with sound making. I find my voice triggered by the dance/movement I observe and breathe with, during my guiding of classes or workshops, and by the tunes and rhythms of the musicians I play with. In context of the Group Motion workshops, my voice reaches into and connects with the energy of the dance, in support and exchange of its dynamic flow and directive undercurrent.

My engagement in music has always been there, almost without myself noticing, and without effort, rather like a constant companion, and the impact becoming known to me by the comments of others. My sense of pitch is more like that of a bird who doesn't know an A from a C, yet always hits the right tone. It is not from a conscious decision, but rather from an innate knowing and my sense for providing support and harmony, regulated by breath.

I believe it stems from growing up in a family of musicians—throughout my childhood years I was listening to my mother, a pianist, teaching piano, my aunt an opera singer, practicing her voice, my uncle, the First French Horn player of the symphony orchestra, practicing for concerts, my sister, a music teacher, practicing flute. I assume the invisible voice while listening to all, finding my voice within it. Now, I still find my voice, or rather, whether in harmony or dissonance, my voice finds itself. My music playing also includes rhythm playing drums and percussive instruments. Throughout the years, I have noticed the healing effect of sound making on myself and others, and have researched such practices since the early 1980s.

* * *

Manfred—I was supposed to become a musician. Between age 7 and 14, I studied playing the violin, and the piano. I sang with my whole family in the Bach choir, and I even took a stab at organ playing. That all stopped when I was uprooted, and had a total change of life when I moved to live and go to school in the big city of West Berlin. My music studies could not continue, and soon I totally abandoned the idea that I could ever be a musician if I could not study and practice any more.

It was many years later, in the context of working with dance, that I reengaged with music, and the way back in for me was the discovery of the synthesizer. I was able to make the electronic music breathe with the dance at the throw of a switch, partly because by that time I was a dancer myself. I have been playing and composing music for dance since then, and particularly developing the art of playing and leading through the music in the Friday Night Workshops.

Playing with the dance is a form of trance, watching the individual dancers or the groups while I am playing with a sense of them playing me, or me playing them ... along with the other musicians that might be playing. It is at its highest when it is without thinking what scale or what setting to play, when I feel my jaw dropping and my mind disappearing in my fingers and hands, who know where to go and all the tones and intervals and melodies and rhythms I ever heard and knew, from Bach to Miles Davis the Gregorian Chant to the African songs, from Ravi Shankar's ragas to Stockhausen's soundscapes find their way into the music that is completely new and unheard as the dance is new and unseen before. Am I a musician now? I am a dance/music player. It is difficult for me to play music without dance anymore.

* * *

Brigitta—You are still, your senses open, listening with your whole being—as you start moving, your body is following the commands inside of you, drawing into the space the sounds and rhythms you feel or hear. Movement and music have the same breath. Everything is a matter of balance—the balance in your own body, between one another, between dance and music, performers and audience. Everything and everybody has a say through the energy flow of the moment. The space is defined as a vacuum, the bodies like in a test for a new time, are entering, and trying to leave their names behind. The audience is testing their own perception. The musicians, with their instruments, the sound or light technicians at their switchboards, steering, landing, taking off and giving power at the right moment, leaving their bodies behind, letting their soul sounds travel freely between different times.

The dancers are waiting for their souls to take the lead and to carry their bodies through, around and together. All are one, balancing each other's impulses, letting it happen, letting go of thoughts, anticipations, fear, the ego—taking the risk of either staying behind or letting go—visiting one place or many, meeting oneself and becoming others, being held or free, dancing, celebrating their physical and spiritual existence peacefully.

* * *

When the wind blows into the tree, who is singing, who is dancing?
The conductor in front of the orchestra dances.
The musician is moved to move while playing.
The dancer is moved to sing out, while dancing,
To stamp the feet to clap the hands.

Music and dance ... where does one end and the other begin?
Like two beings in the entanglement of making love,

Dance and music, two different manifestations of uniting,
   ecstatically breathing together,
Moment for moment, flowing together, rising, sinking, accelerating, slowing
Being together even in stillness, for that stillness is nothing other than
   a transparency to Let the unheard music, the unseen dance shine through.
It is magic. When both are surrendered to each other, to the flow of energy
The music is becoming the dance, the dance is becoming the music.
One is not doing it.

One is being done by the force of love
That comes through the other,
Two are becoming one. That oneness is so strong,
That anyone who experiences it will merge with it,
With the song/dance, the dance/song of that love.

—Manfred

A Process of Collective Creation

Manfred—The work of the Group Motion Company lives with improvisation in the creation and in the performance practice. The Group Motion structures and games are at the core of it. This process is a collective ritual out of which the pieces evolve. The choreographer/director is the facilitator and organizer who edits and arranges the pieces. The work process will focus on a thematic frame or subtext, then the movement phrases, textures, or spatial organizations are created collectively from structures that fit or enable the particular task. The movement vocabulary does not rely on a particular technique, be it release technique, or ballet, or a specific modern technique, but is organically created from both the choreographic vision of the director, as well the creative responses of the dancers to the proposed structure or thematic focus, and from the dancers impulses and responses to each other in the improvisational rehearsal or performance process. The dancers experience and develop the practice of dancing with each other, not just next to each other. They practice how to sense, read, feel and listen to each other, and make choices from this shared physical, emotional and energetic space of co-creation.

While most of the movement sections developed in the rehearsal process found their set choreographic form and place in the performance, others remained improvised within the structure of the pieces. In special cases of larger dance theater works, the dancers were individually engaged as choreographers, setting particular sections of the pieces. Similarly, the engagement with music and media is an additional collaborative process between the artists involved, as the material is developed, and either set or improvised, integrated in the particular conceptual theatrical frame or thematic focus of the piece. In some cases, the collaboration extends into engaging the audiences at the end of performances, whether on stage, or in their seats.

* * *

Former Group Motion Dance Company member, Megan Bridget is co-director of Fidget, a multidisciplinary art platform, and she writes for thINKingDANCE.net. She offered:

> When I started dancing for Group Motion as a company member in 2000, I encountered another way of using improvisation which has had a huge impact on my work and which I am still learning from, all these years later. In Group Motion, director Manfred Fischbeck would give us an idea, theme, or structure to start with. Sometimes we'd work with music, and sometimes we would dance in silence. We would be given an ample amount of time (usually between 10–30 minutes) to dance freely within the given structure. Then we would sit and talk about what happened. The talking was an integral part of the process. This was where we articulated our physical experience into language, and created a shared discourse around what had just happened in the room. Armed with a sense of our collective experience, we would go back into the improv structure and work through it again, and sometimes again, and again. The repetition of the structures allowed our bodies to develop movement material in the moment.

Kathy Rose, Video and Performing Artist, Guggenheim Fellow and Master Lecturer at the University of the Arts reflected on her long time affiliation with Group Motion:

> When I became a member of the company. .. I witnessed the unfolding of design in their works, which had a very positive affect on me. Structured improvisation was used in a lot of the choreography—some of which required some real bravery in performance. I am thinking especially of *The Great Theater of Oklahoma*; in particular a scene where we had a very dynamic exchange of movement between dancers across a diagonal space, to portray a transformational energy in a molecular or human aspect.

Peter Rose, media artist and retired professor of film at the University of the Arts writes:

> My experiences as a dancer with Group Motion were somewhat abbreviated—I quickly concluded that my contributions as a filmmaker might be the more useful. And thus began a fruitful period of collaboration that brought together Group Motion's refined attention to movement with my own interest in the kinetics of cinema. The synthesis was, in some ways, difficult: film has an easy capacity to upstage live performance, and so the interplay between film and dance required the same kind of collaborative commitment as is taken for granted between dancers. In some sense this was improvisatory—the performative ideas of the company sug-

gested possible film images. These were tried out and modulated to complement the performance, and, in turn, the performance responded to the timing and energy of the images.

And so we tried to work our way though to something of both poetic and political force, the politics arising from the collaborative process, the poetry from the surprising juxtapositions that we found. While most films are typically thought of as generated by a script, our working methods were broader in ambition and addressed visual, kinesthetic, and auditory sensibilities, We had great fun finding our way through to the final work—the process being as important as the final product.

In the earlier phase of the Group Motion Multimedia Dance Company, collaboration was the modus operandi on the level of shared directorship: Brigitta Herrmann, Manfred Fischbeck and Hellmut Gottschild co-directed *Countdown for Orpheus* and *The Great Theater of Oklahoma Is Calling You.*

After Gottschild left the company Brigitta Herrmann and Manfred Fischbeck went on to co-direct *Arrival, Arche Nova, Beyond the Eastern Standard Time, Galaxies in Collision, Mitote, Crossing the Great Stream,* and *In the Garden of Woo.*

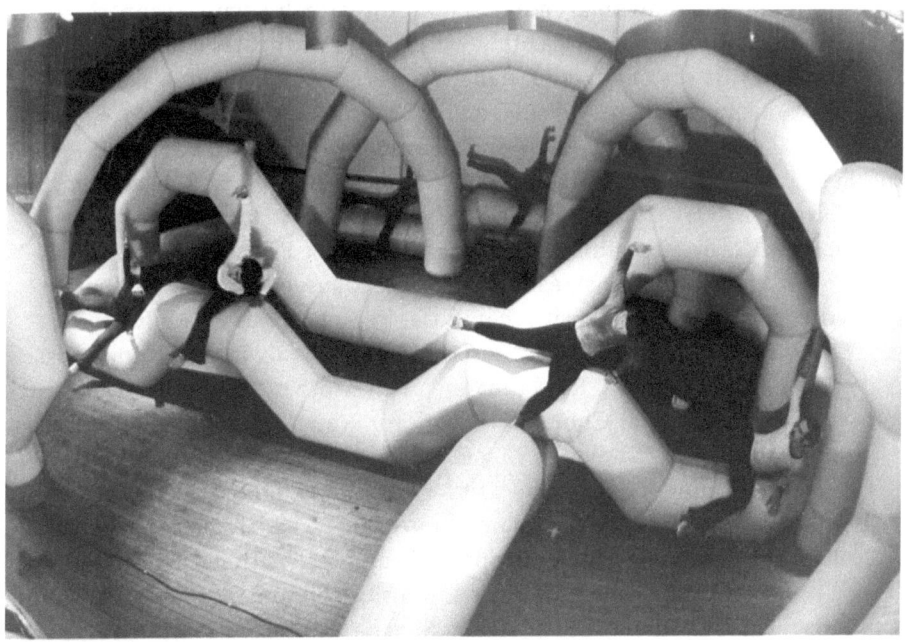

Crossing the Great Stream, company rehearsal picture at Group Motion Studio, Philadelphia, Pennsylvania, 1975. Sculpture designed by Harold Jacobs (photograph courtesy Harold Jacobs).

The thematic frames and theatrical concepts were developed collectively and derived from a wide range of sources and ideas such as myth (Orpheus), literature (Franz Kafka's *Amerika*), evolution and space travel, eastern thought and cosmology and Native American spiritual traditions. Artistic collaborators included: Peter Rose film, Warren Muller film, Charles Cohen music, Harold Jacobs sculpture, Woofy Bubbles sculpture, Alexandra Grilikhes poetry, and Musica Orbis music.

After 1989, both Brigitta and Manfred entered a period of individual directorship and work creation. Brigitta's independent choreographic directorship with Ausdruckstanz Dance Theater evolved a rich spectrum of works and continues to engage numerous artistic collaborators in all media, including: sculptor Joyce DeGuatemala, choreographer Erneste Junge, visual artist Earle Belmont, videographer Fran Markey, musician Toshi Makihara, theater director Darko Tresnjak, war photographer Leif Scoogfors, sculptor; Remo Saraceni, spiritual healer, Djuna Wojton, musician Mark Baechtle, author Barbara Dilley, musician Ron Kravitz, director/choreographer Michel A. Carson, and dancers/choreographers Aura Fischbeck, and Laina Fischbeck.

Manfred's individual choreographic directorship with Group Motion Company produced a series of multimedia dance theater works with collaborators in various media: dancers/choreographers Laina Fischbeck, Niki Cousineau, Heidi Weiss, Jennifer Mann, Myra Bazell, Olive Prince, Laura Peterson, Eric Taylor, Monica Favand, Paul Struck, Either Cowens, Paul Turner, Renee Jaworski, Nicole Canuso, Christy Lee, Megan Bridge, Lesya Popil, David Konyk, Katie MacNanara, Emily Hubler Ramey; actor/director Kevin Augustine; set designer Constanze Fischbeck; sound/lighting designer Jorge Cousineau; visual artist Maureen Drdak, visual artist/writer Quintan Ana Wikswo; composer/videographer Peter Price; composers Andrea Clearfield, George Crumb, David Ludwig, Phil Kline; musicians Lenny Seidman, Ric Iannaone, Tim Motzer, Kenny Ulansey, the Philadelphia Festival Chorus, Network for New Music and the International Alliance of Women in Music.

In the later work period after 1989, the collaborative practice of Group Motion Company expanded into working with guest choreographers and companies, including national and international artists Masaki Iwana, Carol Brown, Rennie Harris, Kenshi Nohmi, Leni Basso, Melanie Rios, Wally Cardona, Oscar Araiz, Silvana Cardell, Deborah Hay, and Susan Rethorst, author of the recent book, *A Choreographic Mind*. In these collaborative engagements with the Group Motion Multimedia Dance Theater, the commissioned visiting artists worked with their own structures and scores of improvisational experimentation, and were able to utilize the company dancers' experiences in this field of jointly realized work.

Community Performance Project

The Community Performance Project is an extension of the Group Motion Friday Night Workshop, and is offered twice each year to engage and celebrate a focused experience of dance/movement and music, as a form of ritual and community. With a different theme for each project, Brigitta Herrmann leads the group to engage in a process of collaborative creation and play to investigate themes based on personal stories, environmental concerns, body image, or dreams.

2004	The Playing Field
2005	Water Works in Motion
2005	Our Body Remembers
2006	Dream Related
2006	The Listening Project
2007	Inner and Outer Spaces
2007	Entranced in Dance in the Life of Plants
2008	Who Was Who Is Who Will Be
2009	Sources
2009	Biographicals and Other Moving Events
2010	Message from the Other Side
2010	Abundance
2010	From Seed to Bloom
2011	Circling Tarot
2012	Beginnings and Endings
2013	Soundscapes
2013	Mandala
2014	Sustain-able Classified
2015	Morphing in Design and Motion
2016	Facing, Dancing ... Through & Beyond Obstacles

Brigitta—Each of these Performance Projects was designed as an 8 to 10 week workshop intensive. We were meeting once a week for 2 to 3 hours. The intention was about bringing people of various media together, in a spontaneous performance event, where all the artistic elements—movement, music, visuals, poetic text—are created spontaneously, unfolding during the process of the event. Interwoven with some of the Group Motion structures, the Performance Project is meant to be a gift for inspiration and exchange, and an opportunity to deepen the experience of dance and music play. All performances are designed to and invite audience participation at the conclusion of the event. It is invigorating to see droves of people excited to join the dance and to see connections being made, friendships kindled, emerging through the dance and an informal, pot luck party.

In "From Seeds to Bloom," we explored elements of air, fire, water, and earth. We embodied these aspects as we moved/danced, sounded/voiced, shared and created together. We asked questions such as: which of the elements do you feel closer to and which would you like to attract into your life? In "Water Works in Motion," we started with reading Dr. Masaru Emoto's book *The Hidden Messages of Water*. With a group of 14 participants and the use of a game sequences, we created movement, poems and a video collage together with live music. We incorporated the structure of the Writing Process, creating poems, along with Traveling Landscapes in order to create the performance score.

Blue—turquoise—transparent hue
Flowing—fluidity
Through me too—————
& through waterberries, watermountains, waterclouds—
Giggling & splashing fairies playing the rainbow
In sacred waterfall
bathing darkness to light

Using those structures as guideposts, it could be created anew each time it was performed. When audience members joined into the dance, we played with forming a line, holding hands, winding, and swirling in wavelike motions through the space.

The creation of Soundscapes evolved as a practice for listening, voicing, moving, tuning in with self and others through movement and voice improvisation. The game sequence incorporated the Doing Nothing Dance, the Receiving Energy structure, the Impulse Games, a practice called Listening Hands, and the Adding Game. We included small percussive instruments into the creation of the dance. We also researched and played with sound frequencies relevant to color.

"The Body Remembers" was a Performance Project with a focus on body image. We used roles of butcher paper, 3 feet wide for a person to lie on and trace their outline of the body. With different color markers, the dancers drew details and marked areas of pain or weakness, areas of cold or warm, tingly or tight. Each participant moved in interaction with her/his drawing to create a movement score. Marking specific areas of the body with arrows, the dancers focused on such area with intention of restoring, strengthening or energizing such part of the body. During performance, the drawings were hung on the surrounding walls. In closing, the audience was invited to travel around, freely gaining access to examine and read the artwork.

In "Facing, Dancing ... Through and Beyond Obstacles," we engaged in visualization to source ideas and stories of obstacles, personal or otherwise which translated into a score and collective creation. The following themes emerged for each of the eight involved dancers as their direction, and for engaging with the other participants to form the creation of their dance.

> Body/mind ... Obstruction
> Hands Tied
> Sleep in Peace
> Escape
> Figments
> Get it done
> I'm not allowed to
> Trapped

In "Sustain-able: Classified," we explored movement and music as a form of sustaining one's ability to be present, and experience one's self in a holistic way. We researched the necessity for people dancing, moving and playing together, as a part of sustainability for the future.

Each of the projects were offered and realized as intergenerational performance projects, and they included an age range from teenagers to dancers in their eighties.

Monday Night Improv Lab

Manfred—The Improv Lab was established as a platform for the advanced investigation of improvisational structures and performance concepts of dance, in collaboration with live music and other media. It invites dancers and musicians with previous experience in improvisation to weekly sessions throughout the course of a season, leading up to performances at the end. This program is conceived and directed as a collaborative process between dancers and musicians using existing structures and scores of improvisation of Group Motion, as well as developing new ones through experimentation.

In the course of the weekly sessions, thematic focuses or contexts are developed, at times also inviting other artists in other media to join in the process of developing a performance ritual. Each of the seasonal sessions works with a consistent body of dancers/musicians, developing a sense of close connection and understanding between the performers. It is the goal to develop an authentic original language of movement and music in the process of working together.

Another frequently applied concept of the Improv Lab performances is the engagement of the audience members, either by inviting them to give written suggestions or material for thematic focuses at the beginning of the performances, or to actually join in with part of the movement structures. With or without direct engagement of the audience, it is essential that the structures and performance scores are made transparent to the audience. How are the choices made, the responses triggered and communicated, how are structures followed or broken, how are themes related to or not, these are the questions and issues to be observed in the performance. Thus, the process of creation becomes as important as the product; in fact it is the product.

Examples of frequently used performative movement/music structures are Group Activation, Tableaux Travel Group Activation, Village Square, Textography, Traveling Landscapes. Most of the Improv Lab performances have been confined to dance/music interactions. Others consisted of extended interplays with other media and art forms:

"I Will Play the Swan and Die in Music" featured music by Elizabeth Hinkle Turner, International Association of Women in Music, and video by Manfred Fischbeck. "Califia and the Trespassers," thematically focused on the abuse and destruction of indigenous natural and cultural sites, featured a site specific installation with visuals and texts by Quintan Ana Wikswo, and original music by Andrea Clearfield. "#shamanic interfaces" involved live interactive video projections by Deija Ti and electronic music by Tim Motzer; "Syria—a Fractal of WE," addressed the Syrian refugee crisis, and involved music and video by Niloufar Nourbakhsh, live music by Tim Motzer, in collaboration with the improvisational score of the dance. Under my own direction, the Improv Lab is invested in the in-the-moment creation of performance as a way of traveling through both conscious and subconscious territories of sensualization and embodiment.

Moving Beyond the Games

Brigitta—From my background with Mary Wigman, I had been taught that improvisation in performance was undesirable and inadequate. In her work, improvisation was the source for inspiration and composition.

> To compose means to build.... The idea, even in its invention, is a gift! But the work of art is creation. It is the artistic deed for which the creator is responsible as much as it is testimony to his being. There are not only the intoxicating moments of conceiving the image. There also is an ecstasy of the sober work.—Mary Wigman, 1966, p.13

I had adopted Wigman's belief for my own work, starting out as a young dancer and choreographer. My dances evolved in search of a feeling that needed to be expressed. I was looking for the urgency, the inexorable impulse or image or both, and wrestling with its definition for accuracy and integrity and clarity. There was no room for doubt or chance. Inspired by the dance work of Dore Hoyer, my early idol and one of the last representatives of the Ausdruckstanz actively performing and teaching, I had modeled my work towards what I perceived as such perfection. There was no room for improvisation in performance. Her work was composed with the most detailed nuances of clarity in all aspects. From spatial arrangement to the dynamic interplay between the dance and music, it was an

Count Down for E, with Brigitta Herrmann, 1986 (photograph courtesy Margie Politzer).

art form comparable to the composition of a painting or a piece of music composition. There was no room for change by the time it was ready for performance.

My outlook and belief has changed exponentially over the time of over 50 years of performance, of experimentation, exploration, research, and studies of various kinds of dance, along with life's experiences and its challenges. Our Group Motion performances were going beyond the games, beyond any structured improvisation, but rather into a surrendering of the moment toward adventure and free flow. I have a dreamlike memory when we, a few members of the Group Motion Company improvised such a performance as part of the Isamu Noguchi installation in Philadelphia. I remember that we entered and disappeared at times in the sculptural setting. Nothing was negotiated before.

Another such even took place at the Cafe Einstein in Berlin. We started, each of us five dancers, at the periphery of the cafe. I remember it was filled with people standing and sitting and with smoke of cigarettes. Smoking cigarettes was still a customary routine. In slow motion, we made our way towards the center and towards each other where the spontaneous dance and music playing began to unfold in surrender to the environment, nonstop for approximately 30 minutes.

I experimented with solo improvisation in performance at various other occasions. At one time, in the gallery at the Moore College of Art in Philadelphia, I was accompanied by my musician friend playing electronic keyboard and surrounded by images on the wall, the audience sitting on the floor and or chairs at the periphery of the space. During this performance, a woman photographer joined me unexpectedly. She moved carefully at the periphery of the space tuning into the dance with her camera. We had never met before. Her presence and the eye of the camera transformed the solo into a duet of sorts, as she became a partner in the dance. How rewarding it was to see how she captured the images in her art, and told her version of the story of this dance.

A solo performance at Movement Theater International, *Someone Is Watching Me*, was in collaboration with live video. The videographer used the camera as the amplifying eye, spontaneously projecting images on the upstage screen, instantly giving the audience access to close ups and inaccessible angles of the dance. He took the liberty to crawl, role, lie down, moving through the audience and on stage. It turned the solo into a duet.

While the Group Motion structures and games are excellent tools for dance movement exploration and initiation into dance, moving beyond the games, breaking the rules leads to exploring new and unpredictable territories of play, emerging into high powered and even ecstatic events. While ritual provides a sense of safety and its familiarity is soothing and comforting, moving beyond the games maybe comparable on a small scale to the adventurer who submerges in the underwater ocean, climbs a mountain, travels the arctic or into space to further an inner and outer exploration. He lets go of an outcome to adhere to the present moment. Such courage may even be a tool for our survival. Moving beyond the games, breaking the rules leads us into the unknown.

How do we practice preparing for the unpredictable? Not unlike swimming in the ocean, the element is the same yet the waves the currants, the temperature are never the same. The practice aims for being alert, being vigilant, exercising sensibility and layers of inner and outer awareness. It is challenging; the mind wants to make provisions for safety. However, in this framework I train to forget the spectacular moments in rehearsal and aim to start from zero. I intend to step on stage with nothing in mind. I empty my mind, knowing the daily influences, the physical, emotional, psychic, social, political have left their traces. Influences of my audience may show up. Going beyond the games is a practice of surrender. I surrender to being vulnerable. Moving beyond the games is an unpredictable journey, often high powered and ecstatic. Whether solo or as a group, we embark on the unexpected.

Reflection on the Practice of Free Improvisation

Manfred—The Seventies brought about a big surge of improvisational experimentation in the U.S.—from Grand Union to Anna Halprin to Daniel Negrin's Workgroup ... from New York to Seattle to San Francisco ... Minneapolis and Philadelphia. There was a wave of discovery leading to entire national Improvisational Dance Festivals on a larger scale, like the one in Minneapolis in 1979, where for a weekend, people were dancing improvisationally inside studios and theaters, or outside on lawns at all times. It was the sign of the times and Group Motion was fully engaged in this process. My sense of recollection tells me that most of the time the improvisations I witnessed or participated in were following scores or concepts, however, totally free improvisation coming with nothing prepared was a rarity.

We had experienced a most radical approach to free improvisation through our encounter with Musica Electronica Viva Roma, I believe we were still in Berlin at that time. They started to play their set with one tone, all instruments at once, for however long it would last, and then entered into the open field from there, sometimes traveling for an hour before "finding the end" together. The total surrender and trust in the moment and each other, no safety net provided, it was like jumping from high flying planes, the only known element being the parachute of one's skill and one's intuition, one's spiritual and artistic survival instincts, finding each other in flight and in landing. There was nothing else to compare with that high.

Over time, it became one of my favorite practices, either solo or with a group of other dancers and or musicians.

That we were able to perform free improvisation on an international tour, like the one to Berlin in 1977, when we traveled with four dancers, Debbie, Antonio, Brigitta and myself, and two musicians Lenny and Ric, was of course a result of many practices together. At times we had a structure, where we listened to and learned from each others' physical and energetic languages, impulses and sensitivities, and were able to call into existence together landscapes of sound and movement that had not existed before.

I remember finding myself roaming underneath the stage of the Akadamie Der Kuenste Berlin in the aforementioned Group Motion performance of free improvisation, at one point, not even knowing how I got there, and bringing back from the "underground" a small plastic tub, that for some strange reason became like piece of a puzzle, a perfect element of the dance at that moment. I remember this as one among many other moments of exits and re-entrances.

Knowing when to be still, when to leave, when to come back, to create space not "use" or occupy space, the practice of listening is at the center of the practice of free improvisation. So is the affirmative, saying YES to each impulse that arises in oneself and the others, and follow it through. When everyone finds an ending together organically, it is sheer magic, actually it is an experience of supreme Knowing.

Another significant memory of a free improvisation journey is the following one: returning to our farm that we lived on at the time, from an all Improvisation Weekend Festival at the Yellow Springs Institute in Chester County, a group of four of us extended the dance, without conscious decision, into our living. This looked like people getting up from a talk or a meal to move outside, alone or together, for as long as was

Reflection on the Practice of Free Improvisation 163

City Dances Parkway, Group Motion Company performance in front of *Government of the People* sculpture by Jacques Lipchitz, Philadelphia, Pennsylvania, 2009 (photograph courtesy Matthew Sharp).

needed or called for, to dance with the sky, with the grass, with the pond, and to return to the house at some point, only to continue dancing-living there. For two days, we experienced a utopia of freedom and surrender to the flow of this dancing and being, to the truth of living fully, peacefully, ecstatically.

Practice of Interaction with Technology

Manfred—Group Motion structures and games of dance improvisation can be described as technologies of energy exchange, that in many instances are equivalent to similar processes in nature: mirroring, flocking, call and response, chain reaction, crystallizing, conducting energy, receiving energy. A similar form of symbiosis is at work in the form of interaction or correspondence with devices of the "new nature" field of technology, technological extensions of the body and computer assisted image and sound making. Group Motion Multimedia Dance Theater was the breeding ground not only for the development of new forms of movement, improvisation in performance and workshop rituals, but also for the innovation of interactivity with new media and technologies. In the company's earlier works it was the use of film as a "moving set" or contextualizing frame for the dance.

While Group Motion's work with film and video projection continues, their discovery and use of new media and technologies occurred in the late 1990s and early 2000s. In Memory Man (1990), I used trigger pads attached to my body as a dancer and hooked up to a keyboard and MIDI controller, so that the touch of hands would trigger the sounds on the synthesizer. I was playing the body like an electronic drum while dancing. At the same time, a wireless mike amplified the singing and speaking, and put it through a voice processor.

In the mid-nineties Group Motion was invited by a computer software company to help develop a computer choreography program that would feature five stick figure dancers on a screen stage, who could be programmed with 25 different "moves" into a dance up to three minutes long. The "computer dance" was then put on video and projected on a screen on the back of the stage, from which a group of live dancers learned the piece and eventually performed it, in sync with the video images. This piece was shown at a technology symposium in New London, Connecticut, where Charles Hartman, a writer who was working with a computer poetry software program at the time, saw the dance. He approached me afterwards with the proposal to write a poetic text for it, based on three hundred words that we would send him. Two months later he sent the text which then was integrated into the performance. It created a mystical, nonlinear layer of words. "The stage is the page of dance," was one of the lines the computer had written, over the already happening magic between the computer stick figures and the living breathing dancers moving in unison. The computer choreography program was rather primitive, I believe it was the first of its kind. The much more advanced "Life Cycle" program that was coming out later and championed by Merce Cunningham was also accessible to Group Motion, and served as a visual score for a much more sophisticated computer choreography in the multimedia dance theater work, "Visitors" (1992). More recently, choreographer David Parsons has entered into interfacing dance with drones.

While Group Motion has not gone to quite such dramatic frontiers, we did make more discoveries of interfacing collaborative creation with new technologies. The most engaging one for me was the discovery of the Sound Beam. Moving and playing inside a 25 foot-long cone shaped, ultrasonic beam that was connected to a keyboard and a MIDI controller, the movement was generating the music. Incidentally, the Sound Beam was developed in the United Kingdom as a device that could enable people with physical disabilities to play music.

Inspired by composer Phil Kline who created the amazing "Unsilent Night" events, where he had hundreds of people carrying boom boxes loaded with audio tapes of his music and walk through the city streets, Group Motion explored the idea of iPods and small speakers attached to the dancers' bodies, and having them move, carrying the music through public sites among audiences who followed them. This, in turn, led to the exploration of "Textography," utilizing the phone as a choreographic device.

The use of Motion Capture has come into Group Motion's practice in the most recent multimedia dance theater production of *(NO)E(XIT)N-TRANCE*. Motion capture, Mo-cap for short, is the process of recording the human or object movement and utilizing the information to animate some kind of data, game, or film. The common ground between the dance and these new media is the interactivity allowing for new dimensions of perception and experience.

When Group Motion was in residence at the Montgomery Community College in 2000, the company was programmed to perform a dance piece that was created in collaboration with Leni-Basso, a dance company from Tokyo that we had met at an earlier residence in Philadelphia. We were able to take advantage of a technology that the theater at the college had available; Internet 2 allowed for simultaneous interactive broadcast of two sites via satellite. At an early morning hour because of the time difference, we were working out on the stage of the theater and—via Internet 2—were able to see our friends on their stage in Tokyo and practice together. It was a truly global experience, and a glimpse of the potential of collaborative dance and music making in the future.

Part III.

Closing Conversations and Meditations

Cooperation: The Universal Creative Principle

Hans Jürgen Fischbeck, physicist, and Manfred's brother—We have considered creative processes in nature and have seen that cooperation induced in critical mass states by microscopic fluctuations is the universal principle of creatio ex nihilo. This principle is demonstrated in nature whenever something new is produced, whenever nothing becomes something, chaos becomes cosmos ... an even higher dimension of creativity can be attained when people succeed in cooperating with one another, when they form a group and construct a "system" which, through the members' complete willingness to delve into one another with their total beings, becomes "critical." With luck, a collective consciousness may then momentarily come into existence; through spontaneous cooperation, this collective consciousness may then create something new, something that transcends the abilities and phantasies of the individuals involved. This is what Group Motion through collective improvisation with game material is looking to achieve in the workshops and the performances.

Dance as a Vehicle for Understanding Human Nature

> The dance is a living language that speaks of man—an artistic message soaring above the ground of reality in order to speak, on a high level, in images and allegories of man's innermost emotions and need for communication.—Wigman, 1966, p. 19

Brigitta—In order to dance, we have to love ourselves, not just our bodies; we have to accept that our feelings, our souls are telling our bodies the right moves. We have to relearn the trust of this relationship. Dance is a language, a direct and perfect possibility for a human being to express him/herself spontaneously. Dance is a medium of the moment. It wants to be perceived in the moment when it comes to life—creating one moment out of the other. The hunger for communication is the drive to dance. As you learn to speak in words by being spoken to, you will learn to dance by being danced to. The instrument is our human body, with all its inner and outer functions—our breath being the secret agent, the link between the visible and the invisible. The principle that we name "love" is the thriving force, a thriving force of life itself. We know this, and we do not need a science to tell us. As we communicate on this non-verbal plane, dancing, our awareness on a micro and macro plane leads us to understand a oneness, a form of unconditional love.

> Love as the absence of fear
> as the absence of competition
> as the absence of pain
> Love is a birthright
> as creativity is healing

I would argue that people will not understand what it means to be fully human, unless they dance. And what I mean by dance is not learning some steps or a style of dance, but the authentic expression of the body, however minute this may be for someone, depending on his/her bodily ability and strength. And it is really about movement, its timing, rhythm, the repetition of something, the effort, as Laban called it. In the framework of dance as a therapeutic process, it can move people to a place they never knew existed for them, to the dance that is. I am so astounded by what shows up, the strength and beauty of people.

The Awakening of the Body in the Technological Age

Manfred—In those cultures and times dominated by ideology, the body was in some ways denied its natural life, condemned as a place of sinfulness or rebellion. This denial at one point led to the eruption of medieval mass trance dances, and in the contexts of ideological dictatorships it was and is used as a vehicle for control, oppression and conformity, as in the military marching or the mass parades in totalitarian societies. Even in the modern democratic Western cultures, dance and movement have been denied the role of a primary language of expression and communication and are placed on the bottom of the cultural ladder. Children do not grow up learning to use and practice it, even though numerous studies have shown how essential the practice of movement and particularly expressive, creative movement are for the development of the whole body/mind.

Recently, this long lasting denial seems to move towards another reawakening of the force of movement and its primary power. We are experiencing, at this time, an unfolding in which movement and dance want to reclaim a more vital role in culture. This comes in the forms of yoga or Zumba crazes, jogging and work out frenzies, new ballroom dance popularity, but also rave dances, break and hip hop dance, "Dancing with the Stars" and "So You Think You Can Dance." Confronted with an exceedingly non-physical, strapped by technology way of living, people seem to want to get in touch with their bodies. But is it only their body, and not also their soul? Dance has been called the language of the soul, as it can speak of the inside, the spirit, the emotional, energetic realities, the space between physical and non-physical dimensions.

Through the ages, everywhere on this planet, indigenous cultures have centered their spiritual practices around dance and the arts, as a practice of survival, of seeking communication with their natural and their spirit worlds, their gods, the invisible forces who seem to rule nature and men. This is true for all the art forms, but dance being the most holistic, naturally and frequently played a central role in the rituals of worship, prayer, invocation and celebration. In contrast, our civilization, after over 2000 years of dominance by major religions, or ideologies such as communism, capitalism, totalitarianism, colonialism, world wars and genocides, the industrial revolution and formation of mass societies and massive migrations, accompanied by ever expanding and accelerating technological advances and an increasingly disembodied way of life, this supposedly most advanced civilization denied dance and the language of the body for centuries as a central and vital role in cultural life.

But as the mind over matter apotheosis of the last hundred years finally seems to be hitting the wall of never ending and intensely deadlier power struggles, with financial and cyber warfare and sense-less environmental self-destruction on a global scale, it appears to become a matter of survival that we come to our "senses," figuratively and literally speaking. We must realize that we can only survive with a conscious mind through matter approach, honoring the life on this planet and this universe in its totality, with its inherent connectedness of the human and all other life forms.

In a new and slowly forming indigenous global culture of the new age that honors and recognizes the earth as the shared home of all, beyond historic nationalistic, racist, classist, gender and ageist cultural and linguistic divides, a new language seems to want to arise, growing from ancient roots. Dance/music and art making are emerging as primary rituals, as practices of compassion, of healing, of envisioning and dreaming, of peaceful co-existence, and a celebration of wholeness. We see more and more people stepping out of the anonymity of mass existence to express themselves individually and collectively, creatively and artistically, through Facebook messages and other social media, through music/art making on their computers or basement garage bands. We see more and more people jogging in the streets, or carrying their yoga mats on their bikes to daily practices, more and more people, young and old, taking up the practice of various martial arts, the hip hop and break dancers, graffiti writers and rappers of the world engaging in friendly and peaceful competitions across the planet.

It seems ironic that this movement arises or breaks through not during the times of a "back to nature" call of the late 19th and early 20th centuries, but in this the 21st century, that could be identified as the "technological age," marked by a seeming take over and dominance of the power of science and the machine. But, of course, it makes sense on closer look, just as it makes sense that the invention of the atomic bomb activated the peace movement, and the pollution and waste epidemic activated environmental consciousness. The arrival of space travel in the 60s provided another vital breakthrough perspective and vision; seeing the planet from outer space had a transformational effect on the astronauts and everyone who paid attention. It provided a physical view of the larger space and helped to invoke global consciousness on one hand, and on the other hand, exemplified and amplified our total dependency on technology.

For me, the question comes into the foreground, raised in these contexts of investigation of the "language of the body," what a culture with a fully conscious nonverbal communication recognized and practiced as a primary language would look like, and what the physical, emotional, psychical, social and political effects would be. What might the inner and outer realities of such speaking bodies in an imagined culture of the future be like? What might it look like on the other side—a culture without a body, without physical expression, without dance, music and the arts as we know it?

The "high art" dance forms such as classic ballet and modern dance, of course, still live in a rather insular or elitist place, and are clearly left to the lower rungs on the ladder of cultural appreciation, education and support. I see two reasons: 1) their traditionally stylized language is not embodying the sensibilities and realities of contemporary life, and not providing accessibility to the larger population of today. In fact, it is keeping itself exclusive to the highly stylized skills and aesthetics of the trained practitioners and the mostly white, Western cultural elite. And 2) it is often more concerned with presentation, or restoration, display, entertainment, competition and personal artistic ownership than with communication and expression of life, its common causes and experiences and needs of the human condition.

In contrast, we have examples of new techniques in Break Dancing, Gaga, Contact Improvisation, and Five Rhythms, mixing with old spiritual techniques of Capoeira and Tai Chi, Butoh, and ecstatic dancing. Now it is not unusual to have site specific performances and improvisational dance festivals, flash mobs, dance marathons, and raves, often based on some form of improvisation, which interestingly enough have some sense of "breaking down" and connecting to the body in a new way. The need for change towards making dance available and valued in its most vital and powerful potential, to provide the experience of expression and communication, of wholeness and healing, and with that to help to create and evolve social change and transformation, this need for change is rooted in our relationship to the body itself.

"I need to quiet my mind" is a phrase one can hear more and more frequently, as the social and psychological stresses of our lives are mounting. More commonly available ways to accomplish that are by taking drugs, or to going to physical exertion, or through excessive consumption. Less commonly available are the practices of meditation and yoga or other forms of mind/body relaxation. It seems however, that this cry to get out of the mind is not only about stress release, but on a deeper level it is about the need to express ourselves, to be seen and heard holistically, as who we are and how we feel, outside of the conforming ways of who we think we are or are supposed to be.

When we get emotional we tend to move. Our body breaks into forms of expression that words are not providing, and in this state we become visible, become who we are in that moment. This is the way children naturally claim their presence, by moving how they feel and following their bodily impulses, until they are told to sit still and behave. This is where dance begins, in people, animals and all of the embodiments of nature. This dance of expression is the natural one that we are born with. It is not the one we learn at the ballet bar or other dance lessons, it is the one we know from the inside and since our birth, unless it is suppressed so heavily that we have forgotten how to access it.

This is the dance, not of showing and performing, but of expressing, becoming and being, and it is available to everyone. People will say, "I am not a dancer," or " I have no rhythm." They still breathe and have a heartbeat, which is the universal source of the dance that never left them. Technical movement practices, just like technical writing or speaking practices, will enhance and expand or define our ways of expression and articulation, especially when they are provided at a young age. However, this training only is fully productive if the natural and expressive movement impulses are also given the space of practice in expression and communication, and are not measured with the "right and wrong" rules of technique teaching. On the newly broken ground of a global indigenous culture of the technological age, out of the urgent need to balance the life of body, mind and soul—to create a space for this integration, a ritual space for all people, all ages, all genders and all races—Group Motion was created half a century ago and is still moving forward.

Beyond the Eastern Standard Time, Group Motion Company performance at Zellerbach Theater, Philadelphia, Pennsylvania. Performers: Brigitta Herrmann, Manfred Fischbeck, Lura Hirsch, Thomas Brown and Ken Kulb, 1973 (photograph courtesy Group Motion).

The Art of Dance and Transformation

BRIGITTA: I was just thinking that a human being is a piece of art.

MANFRED: Yes, a work in progress, which brings up another aspect of what we are concerned with—art as a process, the creation as a process, not the product. And since improvisation is a process, it makes available to the observer the opportunity to see something coming to life, rather than something finished and polished. To see life power, life energy that is transparent in it, whenever that happens, to feel the stream of time pulsating through something—the change element.

There is a uniqueness in dance. That the painter is separate from the brush and actual painting, but the dancer is everything in his own body. At the end, the product in dance is not outside. It is what it was. It is over. It's not there. My feeling is that it is the highest goal of art to be able to experience the whole cosmos as a celebration of its life process and to train our perception for that reality. For example, to be able to experience what water is, in its essence, by the heightened expression of the art—of dancing, or painting, or making music, or writing.

ELIA: You mean, by being water?

MANFRED: Being water. Transforming yourself into water. There is, these days a growing awareness of unified being, and knowing or getting to know that we are all connected with everything. And in this age of the discovery of this connectedness, it seems even more important to be able to actually be all these other things. To be able to be that otherness that is all around. And art can be this heightened form of being.

ELIA: But what the audience perceives or identifies as your image might be different from what you intend. You are not trying to copy, but rather you are trying to experience.

MANFRED: That is right. We use the word transformation a lot, as opposed to making something recognizable in a literal sense. Instead of representing the image of water, I become it.

ELIA: Dance does not attempt to portray, but rather to transform. It is not trying to show...

MANFRED: But to be. So we should never call anything a show...

BRIGITTA: But a "be" (Laughter).

MANFRED: We have not yet found a good word for it.

ELIA: Performance? How about Transformance?

The Art of Free Improvisation

When I am preparing to perform, I try to avoid preconceived notions of how I am going to play, what kind of sound I am going to use, an how I will patch the synthesizer. It is a big temptation to get things ready and to think of settings and sounds that I might want to use. But I always find that if I avoid that, it is usually much better. I just keep a mental blankness about what is going to happen.—Charles Cohen, a Group Motion Musician

Freedom from expectations is not a state of mind easy to achieve. It is a balance between knowing and being. It is all too easy to fall into the trap of relying upon what one has learned. The ending of an improvisation often indicates how connected the dance was. If the ending falls into place, then the dancers know they were together. But the dancers do not think about the ending during the dance. They know when it is there, and sometimes it takes them by surprise.

Everything affects everything else. Each breath, each sound, each movement, each stillness has an impact. Dance, music, performers, setting, audience, all are parts of this living experience.

Jazz musicians when jamming improvise without any group preparation, often without ever having played together before. Certain forms, like the blues, or certain chord progressions are familiar to every player, and the traditional musical instruments also provide structure. Improvisation in dance also needs structure to allow dancers to communicate with each other. Our improvisational vocabulary comes from the dance games.

It is important that there are no preconceptions before an improvisation. As in music, the truth of the communication relies upon the spontaneity of the players who must follow their impulses. The scale on the instrument, or the pirouette of the body can be used in improvisation, but when the dancer THINKS about using these things, rather than letting them happen, the immediate, creative impulse is lost. Aware of the many forms they can use, and recognizing the forms used by their partners, the players do not do anything by design. They let it happen.

Free improvisation is a very vulnerable art form. It only works when all its participants are true to their impulses and sensitive to one another. The experience, deep and subtle, where every thought intrudes upon this union of mind, body, and soul, is as fleeting as dreams, and even more so, because it is not protected by sleep.

> MANFRED: Improvisation is like dreaming. It is really free because you are traveling to places with other people where you have not been. And each place is completely real and at the same time fantastic and non-existent, in a sense.
> BRIGITTA: I think that it is like getting away from the consciousness and then getting back to it. That is the similarity between dreaming and dancing.
> ELIA: You have a sense of wakefulness and dreaming at the same time.
> MANFRED: It is dreaming while you are awake.

From Then to Now and There to Here

In August of 2017, Brigitta and Manfred returned together to Germany to lead dance movement lectures and workshops in Marburg and Berlin.

BRIGITTA: What was significant in Marburg was the fact that the event was entitled "Mary Wigman's Erbe in Strukturen Zeitgenössischer Tanzimprovisation," [Mary Wigman's Heritage in Contemporary Dance Improvisation]. It highlighted the connection of Mary Wigman to the Group Motion Workshop, and it made an impact in regard to who came to listen and participate. This never occurred in the United States, where Mary Wigman does not have the same popularity. So, it was putting Group Motion into a remarkable, very interesting context.

MANFRED: We had a wonderfully receptive audience in Marburg.

BRIGITTA: A full house.

MANFRED: People were telling us afterwards, they were very moved by the lectures and the performance. Our daughter Laina and her group came from France to perform a piece, the *Dance of Love* based on the Mary Wigman series *The Seven Dances of Life*.

BRIGITTA: I performed a small part in it.

MANFRED: Then we had our workshop the next day.

BRIGITTA: People were very inspired by the lecture and signed up. It was presented in a good space. Our sponsors from the University did a marvelous job to organize everything and publicize everything, exceptional.

ANNA: Any surprises emerge in the workshop?

MANFRED: One thing that didn't surprise was that the work works. It seems to do that wherever we go. In this group, however there was a degree of receptivity and soulfulness in the way they responded and related to each other. It was intergenerational group, with all levels of dance experience.

BRIGITTA: The focus, the concentration. It was wonderful.

MANFRED: In the closing circle, afterwards, some people found themselves in tears. Amazing.

ANNA: What structures did you use in your workshops there?

MANFRED: Laina did the breathing warm-up, and then we did Triangles, the Adding Games, and then the Dialogue and Trialogue Games. The Adding Game was really special.

ANNA: How so?

BRIGITTA: It was a large group. We had four circles, and then we put them all together, as four concentric rings, each with a theme of one of the elements: water, fire, earth, and air, forming a large Mandala kind of structure.

MANFRED: People really engaged in this experience of co-creation with these structures. I do not think they ever had that experience before.

ANNA: And Berlin?

MANFRED: It was very special as well. We presented the final part of a weeklong dance workshop at a major dance center, given to a group of dancers from South Korea. Our daughter Aura gave a warm-up focused on breathing and contact.

BRIGITTA: There were ten young women, very well trained, a good range of experience. It was interesting to see, they did speak some English, not a lot, and not everyone understood.

MANFRED: In Marburg, the workshop was with almost all non-professional dancers. In this case, this group had worked and trained together professionally, all week.

BRIGITTA: The Korean women were more formal, more technically oriented, not as emotionally or psychologically engaged, at least in the beginning, but they were at the end.

MANFRED: It was actually magic, how they broke through to dancing creatively with each other. The fact that it was possible, after a technically difficult week, was so energizing for them.

BRIGITTA: In the beginning, because of the simplicity of the structures, they had a harder time getting into it, but once they broke through, all of a sudden, their own authentic movement came through. And they were smiling.

MANFRED: They were really playing.

BRIGITTA: Really playful.

MANFRED: The next day, in another session with the same group in Berlin, they were joined by some additional Berliner dancers, and three children.

ANNA: How old?

MANFRED: Ages twelve, ten, and, how old was the little one, four?

BRIGITTA: Five. He was five.

MANFRED: Ah yes. They all had danced before with their moms. Two had done Group Motion Workshops before. They lit up the South Korean dancers, helped them get out of their dancers' heads, and got them to be there, fully. At the end, we did the Shadow Dance; it was like a wave of joyful co-creation. It really got them out of their heads and into their bodies.

BRIGITTA: It was totally affirming of the accessibility of it.

ANNA: The accessibility of it.

MANFRED: We couldn't have asked for more.

Dance as an Art Form

Brigitta—Dance for me is manifold, an art form, a way of being, a medicine. The seeds of dance belong to our innate wisdom. The art form is the space to bring forth the yet unseen. The body as a fine tuned, powerful instrument that is capable of reaching into depth and nuances of the human experience. Dance is universal to all human beings, capable of speaking, articulating, drawing into the space, making space and time and energetic dimensions visible. Nurtured by continues practice, by self-observation, by study and determination the seeds of dance can grow and bloom into divine beauty.

Dance technique is given to us to train our bodies—to tune, to sensitize, to strengthen and stretch, to experience the body physically. Throughout dance history, many techniques developed, conveying a certain image of the dance and the dancer, creating beautiful choreographies around the world. They are, in their essence, completed puzzles, perceptions of real information. True choreographies are gifts of grace, and therefore give the experience of grace.

The word grace is always associated with dance—is inseparable from it—but what makes the dance graceful? What is grace? Horses galloping by, stopping, galloping again, do they think, yesterday we were galloping here also? No, as it moves them to run, they do, and are fully within their doing in the joy of it. This is grace. The impulse of the moment is what moves through and becomes form. Grace, we are pulled toward it naturally, wherever we are. It is the beauty that doesn't think of being beautiful, but just is.

Of course, there is dance and there is DANCE and they aren't all alike. I refer to dance as giving space and guidance to find your own dance, and to empower authenticity. What is so special about this kind of dance is its holistic nature, a physical, emotional, mental, spiritual and social activity, a nonverbal language that can reach deep into the subconscious layers of the individual and connect us to others. As such, it does not appear to be a form of exercise, yet it provides the benefit of exercise, rewarding the entire network of systems, circulatory, respiratory, muscular, skeletal, endocrine, nervous, and while it is balancing the body, mind, emotion, and spirit, it is fun.

The ability to create dialogue through interactive structures, and to function in small and in large groups goes beyond the common understanding of dance performance. Group Motion's emphasis on awareness and the facilitation of intuitive learning supports a visual, auditory, and kinesthetic sharpening of perception to self and in relation to other, fostering well-being and physical, emotional, and spiritual growth, through rhythm, synchrony, expression, vitalization, cohesion, integration, and symbolism.

This form of dance making is available to everyone for re-creation, transformation, healing, harmonizing, balancing, and for play. We can enter into a state of being present, inner knowing, or wisdom. We let go of ego, so to speak, we "lose our minds," and gain another sense of self-consciousness. In doing so, we facilitate the balance of left brain with right brain, the rational with the intuitive. I believe that the ability and practice of this form of dance is a catalyst for health, for the survival of the human race.

Dance Is a Way of Life

Manfred—I watch the children—they like to move. They run when they feel like it. They lie down in the middle of the room. They skip through the supermarket. They sit under a chair. They climb on each other when they feel like it. They follow the flow of their energy with their whole bodies. What grace. I watch them and I envy them. And I realize that in me there are impulses to move, that my body, if I would let it go, would follow them.

And I watch the "crazy" people in the streets—I watch them do their strange dances, their strange songs. One side of me wants to pity them, the other experiences grace there too, the grace of a strong energy manifesting itself in their bodies.

Don't we sometimes just feel like running or skipping, or lying down, or standing still, or swaying—but we can't do it? The rules of social behavior don't allow it. And haven't we all experienced the incredible feeling of energy release whenever we did move, whenever we let our bodies speak and listen, letting dance be a way of life?

Part III. Closing Conversations and Meditations

> Wise men speak of wonder and worlds into infinity
> Of worlds I only know but two
> A dying world and a dancing world
> And a dancer I would be
>
> —Elia

Appendix I
Dance Chronology: Brigitta Herrmann

Works of Original Choreography and Collaboration

Unruhe, solo, Mary Wigman School of Dance, Berlin, Germany, 1960.
Olmose, solo, Hochschule für Bildende Künste, Berlin, Germany, 1962.
Haiku, solo, Schaubühne am Hallischen Ufer, Berlin, Germany, 1963.
Ambience, solo, Schaubühne am Hallischen Ufer, Berlin, Germany, 1963.
Whirl, collaboration with Leanore Ickstadt, and Inge Sehnert, Schaubuehne am Hallischen Ufer, Berlin, Germany, 1965.
Six Dances in White, collaboration with Hellmut Gottschild, Akademie der Kuenste, Berlin, Germany, 1966.
Suffle, Ornamente, Glockenduo, collaboration with Hellmut Gottschild, Akademie der Kuenste, Berlin, Germany, 1966.
Stadion, collaboration with Hellmut Gottschild, Inge Sehnert, and Leanore Ickstadt, Akademie der Kuenste, Berlin, Germany, 1967.
Malvena, collaboration with Hellmut Gottschild, Inge Sehnert, and Leanore Ickstadt, Akademie der Kuenste, Berlin, Germany, 1967.
Countdown for Orpheus, collaboration with Hellmut Gottschild, and Manfred Fischbeck, original music: K. Kessler, Thomlinson Theater, Philadelphia, 1968.
The Great Theater of Oklahoma Is Calling You, film collaboration with Manfred Fischbeck, Hellmut Gottschild, and Peter Rose, Philadelphia, 1969.
Before and Here and Now and Then and There, film collaboration with Manfred Fischbeck, WHYY-TV, Philadelphia, 1970.
There Is Going to Be an Arrival, film collaboration with Manfred Fischbeck and Peter Rose, original music by Anomali, WHYY-TV, Philadelphia, 1971.
Galaxies in Collision, collaboration with Manfred Fischbeck and Warren Muller, Shubert Theater, Philadelphia, 1971.
Arche Nova, film collaboration with Manfred Fischbeck and Warren Muller, music by Charles Cohen, Zellerbach Theater, Philadelphia, 1973.
Beyond the Eastern Standard Time, film collaboration with Manfred Fischbeck and Warren Muller, Zellerbach Theater, Philadelphia, 1974.
Mitote, film collaboration with Manfred Fischbeck and Warren Muller, original music by Musica Orbis, Shubert Theater, Philadelphia, 1974.

Crossing the Great Stream, Evening length work, Eight dancers, Multimedia production, collaboration with sculptor Harold Jacobs, inflatable sculpture; original music: Marshal Taylor, Charles Cohen, Ron Thomas, Manfred Fischbeck; co-direction. Academy of Music, Philadelphia, 1975.

Landing on the Blue Plain, collaboration with Alexandra Grillikhes, original music by Charles Cohen in collaboration with Manfred Fischbeck; Yellow Spring Institute for the Arts, Yellow Springs, Pennsylvania, 1976.

Between Heaven and Earth, seven dancers, performed with the accompaniment of the Philadelphia Orchestra playing Bach's "Little Fugue in G-Minor," Academy of Music, Philadelphia 1977.

Live Story, five dancers, multimedia production in collaboration with Manfred Fischbeck, Harold Prince Theater, Philadelphia, 1978.

Breathe, five dancers, Schubert Theater, Philadelphia, 1979.

The Garden of Woo, eight dancers, collaboration with Woofy Bubbles [costumes], and Manfred Fischbeck, commissioned by the Philadelphia Orchestra, Academy of Music, Philadelphia, 1979.

Impulses of the Heart Time & Imaginary Landscapes, collaboration with Woofy Bubbles and Manfred Fischbeck, original music by Lenny Seidman, Academy of Music, Philadelphia, 1979.

Have a Talk with God, College for the Performing Arts, Philadelphia, 1979.

Reflection on the Planet, eight dancers, collaboration with Manfred Fischbeck and Tonio Guerra, original music by Lenny Seidman, commissioned by the Yellow Springs Fellowship for the Arts, Yellow Springs, Pennsylvania, 1980.

Wakedreams, dance and music improvisation with Manfred Fischbeck, Lenny Seidman, Ric Iannacone, Ric Schachtebeck, and Tonio Guerra, Cafe Einstein, Berlin, Germany, 1980.

Earthlings, six dancers, multimedia production, Yellow Springs Institute for the Arts, Yellow Springs, Pennsylvania, 1980.

Masc Piece, solo, Dance Week at the Painted Bride Arts Center, Philadelphia, 1980.

Orbit, with original music by Charles Cohen and Ric Iannacone, commissioned by the Yellow Springs Fellowship for the Arts, Yellow Springs, Pennsylvania, 1980.

In Love with the Moment, with original music by Charles Cohen and Ric Iannacone, commissioned by the Yellow Springs Fellowship for the Arts, Yellow Springs, Pennsylvania, 1980.

In Love with the Moment and Breath Spaces, improvisation in performance with Debora Butler, Manfred Fischbeck, Tonio Guerra, Brigitta Herrmann, Ric Iannacone, and Lenny Seidman, Akademie der Künste, Berlin, Germany, 1980.

Internuncius, solo, Philadelphia, 1984.

Mandala, sixteen dancers, University of Pennsylvania Dance Co., Philadelphia, 1982.

Mitote II, six dancers collaboration with The New Music group of Philadelphia, Schubert Theater, Philadelphia, 1983.

Someone Is Watching Me, solo, collaboration with Fran Markey, live video, Group Motion Studio Theater, Philadelphia, 1985.

The Circus, Children's Production, Group Motion Studio Theater, Philadelphia, 1986.

The Missing Piece, Children's Production, Meredith School, Philadelphia, 1986.

Countdown for E..., ten dancers, multimedia production, collaboration with Trip Denton, video, Conwell Theater, Philadelphia, 1986.

Excuse Me, I Have to Make a Phone Call, seven dancers, collaboration with Remo Saracini [cybernetic phone booth], and Fran Markey [videography], Painted Bride Arts Center, Philadelphia, 1987/88.

Dance Chronology: Brigitta Herrmann

Handmaiden and the Lyric, seven dancers, collaboration with Djuna Wojton, Group Motion Studio Theater, 1987.
Turning Point, solo, collaboration with Leif Skoogfors [slides], Group Motion Studio Theater, Philadelphia, 1988.
Pillows, six dancers, Drake Theater, Philadelphia, 1988.
They Dance Alone, duet, collaboration with Michael A. Carson; Drake Theater, Philadelphia, 1989.
Once Bitten Twice Shy, duet, collaboration with Michael A, Carson; Painted Bride Arts Center, Philadelphia, 1989.
Invitation to Stillness, solo, collaboration with videographer Fran Markey and Mark Baechtle on synthesizer, Mandell Theater, Philadelphia, 1990.
Imprints, seven dancers, Painted Bride Arts Center, Philadelphia, 1990.
Hochzeitstanz, duet, collaboration with Michael A. Carson, original music by Mark Baechtle, poetry by Hanna Wallace Painted Bride Arts Center, Philadelphia, 1990.
Bare Essentials, seven dancers, Movement Theater International, Tabernacle Theater, Philadelphia, 1991.
Between a Door and Its Hinges, duet, collaboration with Darko Tresnjak, Painted Bride Arts Center, Philadelphia, 1992.
Earthmatters, six dancers, commissioned by WHYY-TV, Spot Light Series, Philadelphia, 1992.
Entrance to Heaven, twelve dancers, original music by Mark Baechtle, Movement Theater International, Tabernacle Theater, Philadelphia, 1993.
Between Heaven and Earth, solo, Mary Wigman Festival, Dresden, Germany, 1993.
The Cat, solo, Movement Theater International, Tabernacle Theater, Philadelphia, 1994.
The Danger of Eating, five dancers, original music by Toshi Makihara, Conwell Theater, Philadelphia, 1994.
Sincerely Yours, four dancers, Movement Theater International, Tabernacle Theater, Philadelphia, 1995.
Earthmatters, nine dancers, collaboration with Joyce de Guatemala [hand-painted river rocks], Arts Bank, Philadelphia, 1996.
Desert Flowers, thirteen dancers, collaboration with Earle Belmont [visual artist], Arts Bank, Philadelphia, 1996.
Open the Doors, six dancers and two musicians, collaboration with German choreographer Erneste Junge, Osnabrück, Germany, 1996; Kumquat theater, Philadelphia, 1997.
Invocations, five dancers and two musicians, collaboration with sculptor Joyce de Guatemala, German choreographer Erneste Junge, and guest artist Laina Fischbeck,, outdoor performance in Glenmore, Pennsylvania, 1997.
Emergence solo, collaboration with Jorg Cousineau [set and slide installation], Kumquat Theater, Philadelphia, 1998.
Golden Bird, four dancers, Kumquat Theater, Philadelphia, 1998.
Mandala, four dancers, Drake Theater, Philadelphia, 1999.
Internuncius, solo, Festival au Vieux Saint-Etienne, Rennes, France, 1999.
Years, Months, Days Between Us duet, collaboration with Aura Fischbeck, Chautauqua Community House, Boulder, Colorado, 2000.
Metamorphosis, seven dancers, Naropa University, Boulder, Colorado, 2000.
Moods of a Dream, Performing Arts Center, Naropa University, Boulder, Colorado, 2002.
About Time, solo, Naropa University, Boulder, Colorado, 2002.

Landing, solo & four dancers, Naropa University, Boulder, Colorado, 2002.

Wandering Mind & Matter, solo & three dancers, performance and video documentation for Temple University Dance Archive, performed at Conwell Dance Theater, Philadelphia, 2003.

Who Are You, Solo, as part of Oracles, an Evening Length Program by Group Motion Dance Company; Drake Theater, Philadelphia, 2004.

Beyond the Eastern Standard Time (Reconstruction of the original choreography from 1973) five dancers, collaboration with Manfred Fischbeck, for Group Motion Company's 35 Anniversary performed at the Arts Bank, Philadelphia, 2004.

The Playing Field, 16 dancers; a Group Motion Community Performance Ritual in collaboration with Manfred Fischbeck, Chambers Wiley Memorial Church, Philadelphia, 2004.

Water Works, Group Motion Community Performance/Ritual, CEC, Philadelphia, 2005.

The Body Remembers, fifteen dancers, Group Motion Community Performance Ritual, CEC, Philadelphia, 2005.

The Passion for Dance: In the Spirit of Mary Wigman, seven dancers/choreographers, honoring Mary Wigman's 120th birthday anniversary, Meetinghouse Theater, Philadelphia, 2006.

In the Circle, Ausdruckstanz: Imprints in Motion, Meetinghouse Theater, Philadelphia, 2006.

The Listening Project, Group Motion Community Performance/Ritual,CEC, Philadelphia, 2006.

How to Comfort Her Soul, Ausdruckstanz: Imprints in Motion, Meetinghouse Theater, Philadelphia, 2007.

Physiognomy of the Spirit, thirteen dancers, Meetinghouse Theater, Philadelphia, 2008.

Courage, three dancers, Group Motion Dance Company Home Season Program, Painted Bride Arts Center, Philadelphia, 2009.

War Cry, choreography, Laina Fischbeck, performance D.A.E.D Company; ELABO, Rennes, France, 2011.

About Choice, solo, choreography and performance, Spiel Uhr, Meetinghouse Theater, Philadelphia, 2012.

I Jumped Into Some Animal's Throat, solo, Group Motion Home Season; Performance Garage, Philadelphia, 2013.

The Dance of Longing, choreography collaboration with Laina Fischbeck, Marco Carollo, violin, dance performance, Laina Fischbeck, Meetinghouse Theater, Philadelphia, 2014.

SUSTAIN—able: d—classified: Five intergenerational dancers, Performance/Ritual, CEC, Studio, 2014.

No One Would Care, Jessica Rudman, music, Spiel Uhr, Meetinghouse Theater, Philadelphia, 2014.

Morphing in Design & Motion, six dancers, Community Performance Ritual, Meetinghouse Theater, Philadelphia, 2015.

Facing…Moving Through & Beyond Obstacles, six dancers, Community Performance Ritual, Meetinghouse Theater, Philadelphia, 2016.

Appendix II
Theater and Dance Chronology: Manfred Fischbeck

Theater 1962–1967

Orphee, Jean Cocteau; Ruediger Tuchel [director], Manfred Fischbeck [actor and co-director].
The Good God of Manhattan, Ingeborg Bachmann; Ruediger Tuchel [director], Manfred Fischbeck [actor and co-director].
The Dumb Waiter, Harold Pinter, Ruediger Tuchel [director and actor], Manfred Fischbeck [actor and assistant director].
Dead without Burial, Jean Paul Sartre; Ruediger Tuchel [director] Manfred Fischbeck [actor and assistant director].
In the Jungle of the Cities, Bertold Brecht; Ruediger Tuchel [director], Manfred Fischbeck [lead actor and co-director].

Actor in Film and Theater

A Degree in Murder, Volker Schloendorff, Director, Verlag Houwer, Germany, 1967.
Saved, Edward Bond; Peter Zadek, Director, Volksbuehne Berlin Germany, 1968.

Director in Theater

No Exit, Jean Paul Sartre; Theater Department, University of the Arts, 1998.
Metamorphosis—Franz Kafka; Theater Department, University of the Arts, 1999.

Dance and Dance Theater: With Group Motion Berlin and Group Motion Philadelphia, In Collaboration and Co-Direction with Brigitta Herrmann and Helmut Gottschild (1966–1969)

Countdown für Orpheus, Motion Berlin, dramaturgy, film and text, 1967.
Countdown for Orpheus, with Group Motion Media Theater, Philadelphia, and

Jacobs Pillow; dancer and co-director with Brigitta Herrmann and Hellmut Gottschild, 1968.
Talk, duet with Hellmut Gottschild.
The Great Theater of Oklahoma Is Calling You, Philadelphia and New York, dancer and co-director with Brigitta Herrmann and Hellmut Gottschild, 1969.

Works with Group Multimedia Dance Theater in Co-Direction with Brigitta Herrmann (1972–1989)

Arrival, with Peter Rose, film, WHYY, Philadelphia, 1972.
Arche Nova, with Warren Muller, film, Zellerbach Theater, Philadelphia, 1973.
Beyond the Eastern Standard Time, with Warren Muller, film, Zellerbach Theater, Philadelphia, 1974.
Galaxies in Collision, Shubert Theater, Philadelphia, 1974.
Mitote, Group Motion Studios with Musica Orbis, Shubert Theater, Philadelphia, 1974.
Crossing the Great Stream, Group Motion Studio, Philadelphia and Akademie Der Kuenste, Berlin, 1975.
Landing on the Blue Plain, Group Motion Studios with Alexandra Grilikhes' poetry, Zellerbach Theater, Philadelphia, 1976.
Before and There and Here and Now and Then, WHYY-TV, Philadelphia, 1978.
Life Story, Harold Prince Theater, 1978.
In the Garden of Woo, Academy of Music, Philadelphia, with Woofy Bubbles, 1979.
Reflections on the Planet, Yellow Springs Institute, 1980.
Anima, Yellow Springs Institute, 1980.
Wakedreams, Cafe Einstein, Berlin, and Akademie Der Kuenste, Berlin, with Ric Iannacone and Lenny Seidman, music, 1980.

Works with Group Motion Multimedia Dance Theater Between 1987–Present: Choreography and Direction

Artificial Paradise, with Joseph Wong, Shubert Theater, 1987.
Songs of Guilt, University of the Arts, with John Heijduk, 1987.
Window, Group Motion Studios and Painted Bride, Philadelphia, 1988.
Memory Man solo dance, Group Motion Studios, and Movement Theater International, Philadelphia, 1988.
The Unexpected, with Tom Porett, film, Painted Bride and Group Motion Studios, Philadelphia, 1988.
The Traveling, film, Painted Bride and Group Motion Studios, Philadelphia, 1988.
Diary of Justyna, in collaboration with Andrea Clearfield [music], Silvana Cardell [choreography], The Philadelphia Festival Chorus, Movement Theater International, Philadelphia, 1989.
Hotel del Cuerpo Vivo, with Charles Cohen [music], University of the Arts, Philadelphia,1990.
Global Village, Shubert Theater, 1990.
Silent Winds, with Ramson Lomatewama [poetry], Group Motion Studios, MTI, Philadelphia and Teatro Cervantes, Buenos Aires, 1991.

Body, Group Motion Studios, Philadelphia, 1992.
Inroads, Movement Theater International, and Potsdam Germany and Teatro Cervantes, Buenos Aires, 1992.
Visitors, Movement Theater International, Philadelphia and Potsdam, Germany, 1993.
Computer Dance, with Charles O. Hartman [text], Merriam Theater, Philadelphia, 1994.
Labyrinth, Painted Bride, Philadelphia, 1993.
Labyrinth in the Fourth Court, Arts Bank, Philadelphia, 1994.
Cities, Arts Bank, Philadelphia and Hellerau Theater Dresden, Germany, 1995.
Cyprus Trilogy, Arts Bank Philadelphia and Messina Arts Center, Cyprus, 1995.
Oracles, Fringe Festival, Philadelphia, 1977.
Spaces, with Tobin Rothlein, film; Painted Bride and Arden Theater, Philadelphia, 1998.
Orte (Recalling Hereafter), with Tobin Rothlein, film; Arts Bank, Arden Theater, Philadelphia and Rennes, France, 1999.
From Here to Now, Arts Bank and Wilma Theater Philadelphia, 1999.
Car with Ric Iannacone, and Soundbeam, Drake Theater, Philadelphia, 2000.
Screens, Arts Bank, computer dance video, Manfred Fischbeck, Jorge Cousineau, music, Philadelphia, 2000.
The Running, Arts Bank and Drake Theater, First Person Series, Philadelphia, 2001.
Cultures and Species, with Peter Price, sound and video, Arts Bank, Philadelphia and International Festival Tokyo, Japan, 2001.
The Magic Flute—An Unveiling, with Peter Price, sound and video, Kimmel Center and Drake Theater, Philadelphia, 2002.
The Speaker, Drake Theater, Philadelphia, 2002.
Quest and Lamentations, Arts Bank, with George Crumb, David Ludwig, music, and Silvana Cardell, choreography, Philadelphia, 2003.
Lung-Ta (The Windhorse), in collaboration with Andrea Clearfield, music, Network for New Music and Maureen Drdak, visuals, University of the Arts and Painted Bride, Philadelphia, 2004.
Light Search, Video Dance, Emily Hubler, dancer, CEC Meetinghouse Theater, Philadelphia, 2005.
Chinnamasta with John Luna, video, Jamil Kosevo, text, Tim Motzer, music, Drexel University, Philadelphia, 2005.
Parkway Dances I and II, Parkway Philadelphia, with Phil Kline and Tim Motzer, music, 2008/9.
Sonic Dances I and II, City Hall and Broad Street, Philadelphia, with Phil Kline, music, 2009.
I Think Not, adaptation of Deborah Hay score, Manfred Fischbeck, Solo, Findhorn, Scotland, 2012, Christ Church and Fidget, Philadelphia, 2013.
The Beauty of Decay with Ballet X, Wilma Theater, Nicolo Fonte, choreographer.
Califia and the Trespassers, in collaboration with Quintan Ana Wikswo, text and visuals, and Andrea Clearfield, music, Christ Church Neighborhood Theater and Community Education Center, Philadelphia, 2014/15.
I Will Play a Swan and Die in Music, International Alliance of Women in Music, Group Motion Monday Night Lab, CEC, 2015.
Awake at Dawn, music by Andrea Clearfield, text and video, Manfred Fischbeck, with Group Motion Monday Night Lab, CEC, 2015.
(No)E(xit)n-Trance, with Tim Motzer, music, and Nic Jushchyshyn, motion capture video, Urbn Center, Drexel University, Philadelphia, 2016.

Transfigured Night, music by Arnold Schoenberg, video, Manfred Fischbeck, dancers Megan Bridge and Beau Hancock, American Jewish History Museum, Philadelphia, 2016.
Syria—a Fractal of We, with Niloufar Nourbakhsh [music and video], Tim Motzer [music], Meetinghouse Theater, Philadelphia, 2016.

Bibliography

Castaneda, Carlos. 1975. *A Separate Reality*. New York: Penguin.
Condon, William S and Sander, L. W. 1974. "Neonate Movement is Synchronized with Adult Speech. Integrated Participation and Language Acquisition." *Science* 183: 99.
Emoto, Masaru. 2004. *The Hidden Messages of Water*. Simon & Schuster.
Jung, Carl. 1966. *The Practice of Psychotherapy: Essays on the Psychology of the Transference and Other Subjects*. (Collected Works Vol. 16.) Princeton, NJ: Princeton University Press.
Keleman, Stanley. 1981. *Your Body Speaks Its Mind*. Center Press.
Laban, Rudolf. 1950. *The Mastery of Movement*. Macdonald and Evans Publisher.
Nachmanovich, Stephen. 1991. *Free Play: Improvisation in Life and Art*. Putnam's Sons.
Payne, Helen. 1992. *Dance Movement Therapy: Theory and Practice*. London: Taylor and Francis.
Rethorst, Susan. 2012. A *Choreographic Mind*. Theatre Academy Helsinki.
Steiner, Rudolf. 1924. (1956). *Eurythmy as Visible Speech: Fifteen Lectures Given at Dornach*, Switzerland. Anthroposophical Publishing Co.
Telesco, Patricia. 2000. *Shaman in a 9 to 5 World*. Berkeley, CA: Crossing Press.
Turner, Victor. 1982. *From Ritual to Theatre: The Human Seriousness of Play*. New York: Performing Arts Journal Press.
Wigman, Mary. 1966. *The Language of Dance*. Macdonald and Evans Publisher. For more information about Mary Wigman see: http://www.sk-kultur.de/tanz/wigman/index.html; http://www.mary-wigman.de/. See also: http://groupmotion.org; http://brigittaherrmanndance.com.

Index

Numbers in **_bold italics_** indicate pages with illustrations

Alley, Alvin 13
Araiz, Oscar 29, 154
Arcosanti 113, **_136_**, **_139_**
Ausdruckstanz 11, 19–20, 29, 154, **_159_**, 184

Bachmann, Ingebord 24, 185
Bausch, Pina 19
Beresin, Anna 2, 176–177
body/mind practices, holistic health 19, 53, 92, 122, 132, 157, 170, 172, 178, as therapeutic 2, 20, 41, 58, 122, 144, 189
Brecht, Berthold 24, 106, 185

Celan, Paul 24
choreography 4, **_14_**, 15–16, 19, 25, 59–60, 62, **_71_**, 84, 90, 92–93, 152, dance chronology 181–188, with technology 164–165
Cocteau, Jean 24, 185
Community Education Center 4, 29, 184, 187
contact improvisation 6, 52, 147, 172
Culberg, Bergit 11

Dilley, Barbara 69, 154

film 3, **_14_**, 17, 24–25, **_26_**, 87, 106; in collective creation 151–152, **_153_**, 154, 164–165, 181, 185–187
First Chamber Dance Quartet of New York 13
Fischbeck, Hans Jürgen 168
Fischbeck, Manfred: biography **_14_**, 20–22, **23**, 25, **_26_**, 27–30, **66**, **153**, **_173_**; in Friday Night Workshop **_123–124_**, **_131_**; theater and dance chronology 185–188

Friday Night Workshop 4, 17, 18, 28, 29; Community Performance Project 155; game use **35**, **36**, **_39–41_**, 48, **68**, **71**, 72–73, **_74_**, 80, guide to 122, **_123_**, **_125_**, 126, **_127–128_**, 129–130, **_131_**, **_134_**, 149; retreats **_136_**, 148–149, 155

game, sequences 121–122; _see also_ play
Gottschild, Hellmut 3, 11, **_14_**, 15, **23**, 25, 27, **_153_**, 181, 185–186

Halprin, Anna 161
Harris, Rennie 29, 154
Herrmann, Brigitta: biography, 8–11, **_12_**, 13, **_14_**, 15–20, **_114_**, **_153_**, **_159_**, **_173_**; dance chronology 181–184; in Friday Night Workshop **_123–124_**, **_131_**
Hoyer, Dore 11, 159

Iwana, Masaki 29, 154

Jacob's Pillow 3
Judson Church 3, 15, 26

Laban, Rudolf 145, 169, 189
Living Theater 13–14, 16, 25, 73

music and dance 3–5, 14, 18, 28, 32, 34, 73, 82, 85, 88–89, 93, 159–160; as connector 127, 132, 137, 146, Cunningham and Cage 109; in Friday Night Workshop 122–23, 126–27; music as cue 121; partnership of dance and music 148–151, 152, 154, 155, 158, 165–171
Musica Electronica/Viva Roma 162

Naropa University 20, 69, 183–184
Nederlands Dans Theater 13

Palucca, Gret 11
play 1, 2, 4, *5–6*, 7–10, 17–19, 21–22, 28, 30; as improvisation 31, 34, 37, *40*, *41*, 42–49, 51–53, 58–62, 65, 67, *70*, *71*, 73, *74*, 77–79, *83*, 84–92, 95, *96*, 97–107, 109, 112–113, *114*, *115*, 116–119, 121–122, *124*, 126, *127*, 129, 132, *133–135*, *139*, 140, 142–144; music and 152 (*see also* music and dance); performance as 155–158, *159*, 160–162, 164–165, 170–171, 174–175, 177–178, 182, 184, 187, 189; as therapeutic principle 145–150

Rethorst, Susan 154, 189
ritual, examples 111–121; Friday Night Workshop 122–131; significance 131–140

Sehnert, Katharina 3, 11, 23, 181
Sinaiko, Elia 2, 7, 29, 174–175, 180

technology and dance 2, 93, 102–104, 169–173
Turner, Victor 2, 189

University of the Arts 2, 19, 28–29, *70*, *75–76*, *83*, 92, 106, 122, 152; dance chronology and 183–187

video 1, 58, 61, 103–104, 118; collaboration with 152, 154, 156, 158, 160, 164, 182–184, 187–188; *see also* film; technology and dance

Wigman, Mary 1, 3, 11, 15, 19–20, *23*, 24, 65, 78, *131*, 158, *159*, 171, 181, 183–184, 189; quotes by 9, 78, 168; related websites 189

www.ingramcontent.com/pod-product-compliance
Lightning Source LLC
Chambersburg PA
CBHW020859020526
44116CB00029B/836